Get Off Probation

by

J Jones

The complete guide to getting off probation.

"The degree of civilization in a society can be judged by entering its prisons."

Fyodor Dostoevsky
Russian Novelist

Your Attention Please

The author is not an attorney. This book does not provide legal advice. This book only explains the author's experience in terminating his probation early. Both the author and the publisher always recommend readers consult an attorney on legal matters. Furthermore, both the publisher and the author believe the information contained in this book is accurate, but readers should not rely on this information. Neither the publisher nor the author can guarantee the accuracy of the information in this book. Always consult an attorney on legal matters.

Get Off Probation

by

J Jones

The complete guide to getting off probation.

Copyright

Disclaimer

"This document is designed to provide accurate and authoritative information in regard to the subject matter covered. It is provided with the understanding that the author/publisher is not engaged in rendering legal, accounting or other professional services. If legal advice or expert assistance is required, the services of a competent professional should be sought."

Source: From a declaration of jointly adopted principles by a committee of the American Bar Association and a committee of publishers.

Both the author and the publisher believe the information contained in this book is accurate. Each reader agrees to use common sense and not to rely upon the information provided in this book. Reader agrees to hold both the Publisher and the author harmless for any information provided in this book. The reader is encouraged to investigate other sources of information about getting off probation, such as other publications, websites and books before making any life changing decisions.

This book contains links for third party websites. The author and the publisher do not have any control over and is not responsible for the contents of third party websites. Please use care when accessing third-party websites.

The author is not an attorney. This book does not provide legal advice. This book only explains the author's experience in terminating his probation early. Both the author and the publisher always recommend readers consult an attorney on legal matters. Furthermore, both the publisher and the author believe the information contained in this book is accurate, but readers should not rely on this information. Neither the publisher nor the author can guarantee the accuracy of the information in this book. Always consult an attorney on legal matters.

How to Use This Book:

To get the most out of this book you should read the first ten chapters before starting to write your Motion to Terminate Probation Early. Next, look up the law that gives judges the authority to terminate probation early, which is in the appendix. Look at specific chapters and the Table of Contents for assistance in writing your motion. Overall, I believe Chapter Ten will be the most helpful.

Get Off Probation

Dedication

I dedicate this book to all the ex-offenders who are trying their best to make it on the outside. I'm also an ex-offender and I understand what you are going through. It's difficult, but your only choice is to work hard and try to make it on the outside. You owe it to yourself, your family and your loved ones.

Keep up the good work. I wish all of you the best of luck.

To say the least, there are numerous barriers ex-offenders must overcome to live a normal life and become productive members of society. Always remember, it is possible to overcome these barriers and have a normal life. America is the land of opportunity. Society will give you a second chance, but you have to take advantage of these opportunities.

Thank You

Also, a sincere thank you goes out to my parents, who stood by me when I was going through my legal ordeal. My parents also attended every court hearing and graciously allowed me to live with them for free when I was on house arrest and trying to start a new life. I will always remember and be grateful for their kindness. I lost everything and they were there for me.

I am grateful for the second chance I was given by society. Everyday, I try my best to be a contributing member of society. I consider myself fortunate to have been born an American. Being born in America is like winning the lottery. My life is good and keeps getting improving.

Get Off Probation

X

"The lesson is that you can still make mistakes and be forgiven."

Robert Downey Jr.
Actor

Note from the Author:

I never liked being on probation. There's nothing fun about being on probation. Every month I had to fill out paperwork and I worried about being sent back to prison. Many of my friends in prison were there because they failed a drug test and their probation was violated. I wanted to be free. You're not free when you're on probation. I had to ask for permission from my probation officer just to take a vacation.

I was always on my best behavior with my probation officer. I also worked hard to comply with the terms of my probation. I wasn't perfect and I made mistakes, but I tried my best. My goal was to get off probation as soon as possible. It's easier to start rebuilding your life when you're completely free.

In many ways being on probation is harder than being in prison. When you're on probation, you always worry about getting into trouble and being sent back to prison. It's stressful being on probation. Also, there's a lot of temptation out there and it's easy to make a mistake and get into trouble.

I describe in detail how I was able to get off probation early. My book includes the law that allows the court to release defendants from probation early for every state and the federal government. Also included is the motion I submitted to get off probation early. Step by step, I explain what I did to get off probation early. The first step is to build a good relationship with your probation officer. Once you have determined that you have a good chance of getting off probation early, you should consult an attorney.

Best advice:

Read this book and contact an attorney if you believe you have a realistic chance of getting off probation early. Hiring a qualified professional is always the best course of action.

You never know what is possible until you try. Good luck with your efforts to get off probation early.

Get Off Probation

"It always seems impossible until it's done."

Nelson Mandela
Former President of South Africa

About the Author

First and foremost I want to state the obvious, crime doesn't' pay. I regret the actions that I took that hurt others and myself. I paid for my actions. It's just not worth all of the stress, fines and possible jail time. We live in the land of opportunity. Other options are available to earn a living.

My friends and family begged me to write this book. To be honest with you, I was reluctant to write this book because I don't want to draw attention to myself or my background. Also, I don't want to advertise the fact that I have a criminal record. I can assure you that my story is completely true. I'll do my best to summarize a long story.

I grew up in a small town. After graduating from college I married the love of my life and moved out West. I worked at a series of dead end jobs. I always kept my eyes open to find new opportunities to have a better life. I dreamed of starting my own business. I desperately wanted to achieve the American dream.

Get Off Probation

I came across what I thought was the opportunity of a lifetime. I had the chance to study a business in another state for a week. This business received the majority of it's funding from the government. The more I thought about it, the more I thought this was the perfect business.

I spoke with a close friend about this opportunity. We agreed to start a similar business. I didn't have any money, but I had a lot of credit cards. We started our business with credit cards. It was harder than I thought it would be. It took months to find the right building, hire the staff and get the business off the ground.

Eventually, the business took off. We were making money for ourselves, providing good jobs for our employees and helping people. Life was good. The business was up and down, but overall it did okay for a few years. We had only one competitor in a very large city. There were many people who needed the services our facility provided. Fortunately, we were able to save some of the money that we made. (We would later use this money to pay restitution and legal fees.)

The business started to deteriorate when the government made it tougher to get paid. We stuck it out for a while, but later sold the business for a token amount to a supplier we owed a substantial amount of money to. I thought this was a win/win situation for everyone. In hindsight, I should have closed the business down. If I had closed the business down, nothing would have happened to me. I never would have been charged with a crime and never would have been sent to prison. You live and learn from your mistakes.

I later found out that close friends had been under investigation and had cooperated on my case to get a better deal. This is an everyday occurrence in the criminal justice system. Yes, I'm guilty of the crime. But usually individuals only have to repay the money they owe to the government. It's very rare for anyone to go to prison for what we did, even in major cases.

I hired an expensive lawyer because I thought I could get off with the right lawyer. I was wrong. (It's easy to spend a fortune on legal fees.) I later ended up spending all of my money on legal fees, expert witnesses and paying restitution. (Paying the legal fees was more painful than going to prison.) I was offered a plea deal, but I rejected it because I thought my best friend would then go to jail.

I was looking at up to twenty years in prison. The judge gave me a relatively short sentence at a camp, house arrest and three years of probation. I was happy, but all of my co-defendants got off with only house arrest and probation. While in prison I realized how lucky I was in comparison to most of the other people I met in prison.

I lost everything that I had. I lost my friends, my wife and everything that I owned. I worried about my case constantly and the stress caused my health to deteriorate. (I'm sure my ex-wife blames me for everything.) My ex-wife is a good person and I regret getting her involved in this venture. This is one of the biggest regrets that I have in my life.

I never thought we would get into trouble for anything. I believe we were doing exactly what many other similar businesses were doing. It's over and I can't look back. I'll never get into trouble again. It's just not worth it.

After getting out of prison, I lived with my parents to complete my house arrest and probation. I stayed out of trouble. I also completed a degree and worked at different jobs. The jobs were just horrible, but it kept me busy.

While I was on probation, one of my co-defendants contacted me and told me that she had been able to get off probation early. I asked her what she had done. After being on probation for less than a year, I asked my probation officer if he would support me if I asked the court for early termination of my probation. He told me it was okay. Next, I wrote and submitted a motion to the court asking for early termination of my probation. To my surprise my motion was granted. I was a free man after only serving less than a year of probation. (Keep in mind, I was fortunate. Generally, you should serve at least half of your probation before asking the judge to terminate the rest of your probation.)

I'm rebuilding my life. Everyday my life is getting better. I'm optimistic about the future. Life is good. I'm grateful for the freedom that I have and cherish every minute of it.

Being incarcerated has had a profound impact on how I view the world and interact with others.

I wish each of you the best of luck in your efforts to get off probation and rebuild your life.

J Jones

Table of Contents

(Note: Alaska, Connecticut, Florida, Michigan, North Carolina and Wisconsin have specific forms you must use to ask the court to terminate probation early. Links to these forms are provided in the Appendix listed under the name of each state.)

Download the following templates at http://www.getoffprobation.com/motion or http://tinyurl.com/getoffprobationfile

Read_First.htm: Explains in detail how to use this ebook and the additional files.

Form01_GOP.rtf: **Defendant's Notice of Hearing and Motion to Terminate Probation.** (Must attach Motion to Terminate Probation Early to Notice of Hearing. Use if the court allows you to schedule a Hearing before filing the Motion to Terminate Defendant's Probation Early.) See Chapter Seven.

Form02_GOP.rtf: **Defendant's Motion to Terminate Probation.** See Chapter Six, pages 33 to 39 and Chapter Ten, pages 53 to 78.

Form03_GOP.rtf: **Defendant's Notice of Hearing:** Use this form if the court requires you to first file your Motion to Terminate Probation before you can schedule a hearing. See Chapter Seven.

Form04_GOP.rtf: **Judge's Order Granting Defendant's Motion to Terminate Probation.** (This is more common in smaller courts. Ask the court clerk or the judge's assistant if you need to write this motion.) See Chapt. Nine, pages 49 to 51.

Form05_GOP.rtf: **Judge's Order Denying Defendant's Motion to Terminate Probation.** (This is more common in smaller courts. Ask the court clerk or the judge's assistant if you need to write this motion.) See Chapter Nine, pages 49 to 51.

Get Off Probation

Words of Wisdom

"Genius is one percent inspiration and ninety-nine percent perspiration."

Thomas Edison
American Inventor

"If you can dream it, you can do it."

Walt Disney

"High expectations are the key to everything."

Sam Walton
Founder of Wal-Mart

"You can never quit. Winners never quit and quitters never win."

Ted Turner
Founder of CNN

"You can have anything in this world you want. If you want it badly enough and you're willing to pay the price."

Mary Kay Ash
Founder of Mary Kay Cosmetics

"All of our dreams can come true, if we have the courage to pursue them."

Walt Disney

"When your desires are strong enough you will appear to possess superhuman powers to achieve."

Napoleon Hill
Author of *Think and Grow Rich*

"The prisoner is not the one who has committed a crime, but the one who clings to his crime and lives it over and over."

Henry Miller
American Novelist

Chapter One

1. Can you guarantee that I will be able to get off probation early?

No, I cannot. Each case is unique. It depends on your background, the crime you were convicted of, your behavior since being convicted, the judge and your probation officer. I cannot guarantee that you will be able to get off probation.

2. Does this book provide legal advice?

No, *Get Off Probation* explains in detail how I was able to terminate my probation early. I always recommend seeking the advice of a qualified attorney regarding legal matters.

3. What type of lawyer should I hire to assist me in this matter?

Hire an experienced criminal defense attorney who practices in the jurisdiction in which you were convicted.

4. How much does it cost to hire a criminal defense attorney to file this motion on my behalf?

America is overflowing with attorneys. Costs vary dramatically. Interview a minimum of three attorneys and try to negotiate a flat fee for an attorney to handle this matter.

5. Are you a lawyer?

I'm not a lawyer. I'm just a regular guy who got into a lot of trouble. I pled guilty to a felony and was sentenced to a federal prison camp. I learned from my mistakes. It was a humbling experience. I am now rebuilding my life.

6. Were you perfect when you were on probation?

No, I wasn't an angel. I tried to be perfect, but I made a few mistakes. I had some heath problems and I quit my job to concentrate on the classes I was taking. I tried my best to have a good relationship with my probation officer. This was hard, because I had a new probation officer every few months.

Another time I went to another state without getting permission. I didn't have a choice. This is something I had to do. Probation officers are busy people and it's hard to get in touch with them on a short notice.

7. Can I do this by myself?

Yes. I wrote the motion by myself. I also submitted it to the court by myself. I couldn't afford an attorney or even a paralegal. I was flat broke. This was a difficult time in my life.

8. Can I get off probation early, even if I committed a serious crime?

It's possible, but you have to work that much harder to get off probation early. You have to be realistic and completely honest with yourself. Keep in mind that individuals who have committed serious crimes have received presidential pardons.

9. Are you angry about what happened to you?

I'm human and of course I'm angry. The anger only brings me down. I try to have a positive attitude. It could have been a lot worst than it was. I was more fortunate than the vast majority of people who are sent to prison everyday. My family was there to help me when I needed it the most. I'm a lucky person.

10. In what circumstances shouldn't I ask the judge to terminate my probation?

If your probation officer has any objections, you should think twice about making this request. An objection from your probation officer is a huge barrier for you to overcome in court. Instead, ask your probation officer what you can do to get him or her to agree to your request to get off probation early in the future. (It would be difficult to get off probation if your probation officer has any objections and shares these concerns with the judge.)

11. Why did you write this book?

I wanted to share my story. Furthermore, I want to let other people on probation know that it is in fact possible to get off probation early.

12. Can you tell us more about your life today?

That's a good question. First, I value my privacy. I do not want to be in the spotlight.   Second, I don't want to advertise the fact that I have a criminal record. I paid the price for what I did. Also, I want the readers to focus more on the message of *Get Off Probation* than the messenger.

13. Briefly, what can I do to improve my chances of getting off probation early?

A. Be current on all of your fines or pay your fines off completely. B. Be a productive member of society. C. Stay away from trouble and anyone who can get you into trouble. D. Make an effort to have a good relationship with your probation officer. E. Wait until you have completed half of your probation period. F. Comply with all of the terms of your probation.

14. Why don't more people get off probation early?

That's the million dollar question. I'd have to say it's because nobody even thinks to ask the judge to terminate their probation early. The judge in my case told my co-defendant that we were the first people who had ever asked her to terminate their probation early. She had been a judge for many years.

15. Why did you want to get off probation early? Is probation that bad?

I never liked being on probation for several reasons. First, in the back of my mind I constantly worried about being sent back to prison. You're not free as long as you're on probation. My probation officer had too much control over my life. Second, I didn't like all of the paperwork every month and the rules. I had to ask permission just to go to another state. This was a nightmare, because I only lived a few miles from another state. Once I had to cancel a last minute trip with my father because my probation officer didn't respond to my request to travel out of state. I wanted to spend time with my father because he's getting older and I want to spend as much time with him as I can. Third, I wanted to get off probation because then I'd be free to start rebuilding my life. I wasn't free as long as I was on probation.

There were many other things I didn't like about being on probation. Once, I had to drive a hundred miles to another city to give a sample of my DNA for a government database. This took my entire day. Also, the visits from my probation officer were always unexpected. My probation officer just showed up and wanted to ask me a few questions. I never knew when my probation officer was going to visit.

I desperately wanted to get off probation more than anything.

16. Once I am off probation, what else can I do to improve my life?

If you were convicted of a state crime, work on having your criminal record expunged.

If you were convicted of a federal crime you want to try your best to receive a presidential pardon.

Set long and short term goals for yourself. This will help you to think about the future.

17. What other advice do you have for ex-offenders?

Stay away from illegal drugs and people who are involved in criminal activity. Always be a productive member of society and work towards improving your life. Maintain a positive attitude, spend your time with winners and avoid negative people. Never break the law again because it's not worth risking your freedom and going back to prison.

18. Do all employers run background checks on applicants?

No, many employers do not run background checks. It's expensive to run a thorough background check.

19. How many Americans have criminal records?

Millions and millions of Americans have criminal records. I've seen estimates that over forty-five million Americans have criminal records. The numbers are just staggering.

20. How do I get a job with a criminal record?

Move to a city that has a low unemployment rate. Make getting a job your fulltime job. Grab the best job you can get. Even if it's working at a fast food restaurant or digging ditches. Your life will get better once you are working fulltime. Earn your GED or go back to school and earn a degree or learn a skill that's in high demand.

21. In your opinion, what are the biggest problems with the criminal justice system?

I wouldn't know where to begin. Books could be written on this topic. Overall, the system is hell bent on incarcerating as many people as possible. (The prison industrial complex provides a good living to the people who are part of it.) There's something wrong with a system that overwhelmingly incarcerates the poor, uneducated and members of minority groups. The statistics speak for themselves.

The American criminal justice system has its share of problems, but it's better than the justice system in most other countries. I'm grateful for the US Constitution and the legal rights all of us are given.

22. What is the greatest thing about living in America?

I love my country. I thank God everyday that I was fortunate enough to be born in America. It's the land of opportunity. America is the greatest country in the world. Everyone is given a second chance. You can achieve the American dream by working hard. Being born an American is like winning the lottery. People from many other countries would give anything to gain entry to America.

Inmates at federal prison camps (AKA club fed) have a higher standard of living than people in many developing countries.

23. What's the best thing about getting off probation early?

I'm a free man again. I can do anything I want to do. I can travel to another state or another country without having to ask for permission. Also, I don't have to worry about screwing up and being sent back to prison. Being completely free is great. I cherish every moment of my freedom. Life is good.

24. Do you provide fill in the blank forms I can use to write my motion?

Yes. *Get Off Probation* includes fill in the blank forms you can use in writing your motion. Go to http://www.getoffprobation.com/motion or

http://www.tinyurl.com/getoffprobationfile

25. Is it difficult to write a motion to terminate probation early?

My book tells you everything you need to ask the court to get off probation early. Step by step the process is explained in plain English.

26. Is it difficult to format a motion to terminate probation early?

It's not difficult to format your motion. The easiest way is to just copy the format of other documents in your case. You can also follow the formatting guidelines in the court rules. Judges generally grant defendants who are representing themselves some leeway.

27. Does my motion need to be 100% perfect to be accepted by the court?

Your motion usually doesn't have to be perfect. Try your best to make it look good. Federal judges have accepted hand written motions from prisoners. (Many prisoners don't have access to typewriters in prison.)

28. Why is your book the best on this topic?

This is the only book there is on how to get off probation early. *Get Off Probation* is written in plain English and it's easy to understand.

I explain, step by step, what I did to get off probation early. Also, the federal and state laws giving the courts the authority to let individuals off probation is included. *Get Off Probation* provides hope to many people that they could possibly also get off probation early.

The motion I submitted to the court to get off probation early was successful and it's included in the book. **Get Off Probation provides all the information you need to ask the court to let you off probation early.**

By reading *Get Off Probation*, you should be able to determine if you are a good candidate to get off probation early or if you need to wait before making your request to the court.

The sooner you get off probation the sooner you can start rebuilding your life. I wish each of you the best of luck in your efforts to get off probation early.

"I like the dreams of the future better than the history of the past."

Thomas Jefferson
3rd President of the United States
Principal author of the Declaration of Independence

Chapter Two
My Story

I will never forget how horrible my life was a few years ago. It was a living nightmare. I was facing criminal charges related to a business I had once owned. The stress was too much for me to handle. I thought many times that I would end up in a psychiatric hospital. I didn't have any energy and my health was going to hell in a hand basket. I took medicine to help with my heartburn. I needed psych meds to deal with the stress and the depression, but I was reluctant to go to a psychiatrist.

"Twenty years. Twenty damn years!" I kept thinking to myself as I entered the court room to be sentenced. Twenty years seemed like a life sentence. Twenty years seemed like a death sentence. We had to wait for my fancy, high priced lawyer, who was always late for everything. The prosecutor didn't even bother to show up for my sentencing and sent one of her co-workers. Eventually, my lawyer showed up and the court came to order.

I was given an opportunity to address the court. I told the judge that I was sorry for everything that had happened and I emphasized that I had made full restitution and the government actually made a profit on my case.

My attorney also made a short speech, I think. It's all a blur as I look back on this memory that I do not want to remember. It was a living hell. I thought I could have gotten off or at least gotten a better deal if I hired an expensive attorney. This absolutely wasn't the truth in my case.

The judge sentenced me to a short time in prison, house arrest and three years probation.

I was smiling and the happiest person in the courtroom. I had expected twenty years. I thought the judge was going to throw the book at me. (My mom thought the judge had been planning on giving me only house arrest, but she became furious because my attorney was late again. He had been late during every other court appearance also.) It's ancient history now. It doesn't really matter anyways.

Next, the judge asked if I had any requests. I asked to be sent to a prison near my parent's house. (I wanted to be close to my family to make it easier for them to visit me.) The judge said she would make the request, but others would ultimately decide where I would do my time.

While I was on pre-trial I was on my best behavior. I checked in with my pre-trial officer once a month in person. I also called once a week and submitted my paperwork. I learned the rules inside out and followed the rules.

While I was out on my pre-trial, I didn't have a job. I stayed busy learning everything that I could about the criminal justice system, prison and the details related to my case. Not having a job was a big mistake. Judges and the system in general doesn't look favorably on defendants who don't work. I most likely would have received only house arrest if I was working at the time of my sentencing. I was foolish for not getting a job and being a productive member of society. This was the second biggest mistake that I had made. (The biggest mistake had been hiring an expensive law firm to work on my case.) My last attorney was a nice guy and graduated from a top law school, but I could have received the same results with a public defender or a cheaper attorney. I could have bought a house in a small town with all of the money I wasted on legal fees. (Once you are a convicted felon it's a hell of a lot harder to get a descent job and make money again.) Wasting money on legal fees may be the biggest regret of my life.

"My client would like to self-surrender in three months. He is currently working towards a degree and would like to self-surrender in three months. This will give him time to complete the semester." My attorney made the request.

"Is three months enough time?" The judge asked.

I nodded. I had the impression that the judge would be happy to allow me to self-surrender even at a later date. I just wanted to go to prison and get it over with and start my life again.

"Motion granted." The judge said with a smile.

It was over. I didn't have to worry about what would happen to me.

We went outside. I still had a few questions to ask my attorney. My attorney just wanted to get as far away from me as possible. I had the impression that he thought I was going to hit him. On a personal level I liked him, but the legal fees would eventually drive me into bankruptcy.

Back Story:

I was offered a plea agreement, which would have guaranteed no jail time. I rejected it immediately, because I'm sure my best friend would have received prison if I had taken that deal. I cared about her and I didn't want anything to happen to her. (Another co-defendant later was offered the same deal and took it. She only received house arrest.) I was angry. I thought the legal system was a joke. For a long time, I was angry. Then I realized my anger was only holding me back. After several years, I have regained a level of respect for the justice system.

I eventually pled guilty to a felony. I had a business that provided services to the public, which the government paid for. My business tried to maximize reimbursement from the government. I never thought I would get into trouble. At the very most, I thought the government would ask for some money back and that would be the end of it.

I later sold my business for a token amount to people I considered to be friends. My friends were under investigation for fraud. They later pled guilty to fraud. One day, out of the blue, government investigators showed up at my office and started asking questions. I was caught off guard and made incriminating statements against myself.

I ended up losing everything. This is common when you have legal problems. My lawyers and the government took everything that I owned. My beautiful wife didn't want anything to do with me. I was truly in love with her. But love has to be a two way street. We were divorced and I was heart broken. I honestly thought many nights that I would be better off dead. This is the truth.

One of my co-defendants was able to keep her job at a large company. She thought she would be fired because she also had pled guilty to a felony. She gave her letter of resignation to her boss, a few days before she was too be sentenced. Her boss immediately tore up her letter of resignation and told her that she could keep her job. She had a good job and earned a reasonable salary. She was also a top-notch employee who took pride in her work.

I wasn't as fortunate. I spent all of my time working on my criminal case. Even though I had a high priced law firm working on my behalf, I never really trusted any of my attorneys. (I had three different attorneys while going through this ordeal. I kept firing attorneys because I honestly believed if I hired a better attorney I could get the results that I wanted.) I questioned everything my attorneys did.

Get Off Probation

The worst thing about going through a criminal case is the legal fees. Everything that I had worked my entire life accumulating eventually ended up in the hands of my attorneys and the government.

I regret hiring an expensive lawyer. My case wasn't that complicated. I should have asked the court for a public defender. I believe I could have qualified for a public defender.

I honestly could have negotiated a better civil settlement with the government by myself. The best deal that my lawyer could work out was for me to pay as restitution to the government many times what I had received. My co-defendants also had to repay a substantial amount of money as restitution to the government. Together we paid the government more than we had received. This might have been a mistake, but we just wanted to do everything we could to make the prosecutor and the judge happy.

I was sentenced to a camp. If you have to go to prison, go to a camp. This is the easiest time you can do in prison.

Prison was better than I thought it would be, except for the food. The food was just horrible. Some days I ate just to survive. I bought Snickers bars at the commissary and this is what kept me alive.

I had one of the best jobs in camp. I was assigned to work in a nearby government facility. I earned 12 cents an hour working on a crew picking up garbage. I was grateful that I could leave the camp everyday.

I met a lot of interesting characters in prison. These are people I never would have met if I hadn't been sent to prison. Overall, this experience made me a better person. Former drug dealers and white collar criminals lived together.

It was like being on a working vacation. The weather was beautiful. There was a track that I walked around with my friends everyday. The stress just disappeared. The law library was great, but the regular library leaved a lot to be desired. I read a book on how to operate a small farm. We were allowed to order books from Amazon. Prisoners have a lot of time and enjoy reading. One of my friends loaned me *Freakonomics* to read. I enjoyed it.

Get Off Probation

I subscribed to several newspapers. My crew collected cans and bottles and our boss helped us trade these in for cash. We used the cash to buy newspapers, Cokes and food.

I'm glad that I wasn't appealing my sentence or facing additional charges. The people who were still fighting were stressed out.

I brought five-hundred dollars with me when I first entered prison. I used this money to buy Cokes, popcorn and candy bars from the commissary. I was generous with my friends. Most of them were dirt poor. My friends, who had been drug dealers on the outside, didn't have anything.

Movies were shown on a large screen TV twice a week. The movies were mostly slapstick comedies. Tyler Perry's movies were popular.

From the beginning, I knew that I had it better than just about everyone that I met. Many of my friends were serving ten years. I didn't meet any big drug dealers in prison. Many of my friends were small time drug dealers. The kingpins rarely go to prison.

I didn't like the weekends, because it was boring. Time went by much faster during the week when I was working. I looked forward to going to work everyday. I never took a sick day.

The camp had approximately 300 inmates. It was near a medium and a maximum security prison. I slept in a small room with twenty other guys. A larger room held over a 150 inmates.

I think being at a camp is like being in the army. My life was very regimented. I was up at 6 AM every morning to eat breakfast. I took my shower after work everyday, because there was a large line in the morning.

I met a few gang members, who were covered with tattoos and looked scary as hell. Everyone was cool. Nobody wanted to get into any trouble, because it doesn't get better than serving your time in a camp.

One of my friends went nuts, after the nurse switched his psych meds. He used a log to bash the head of a co-worker, who he thought had insulted him. (The camp had a few nurses, but didn't have any doctors.)

Get Off Probation

I only got into trouble one time. That's when I missed a count, because I was in the library and the library's loudspeaker didn't work. The guard was angry, but I told him the truth and he gave me a break.

I minded my own business. There was no way that I was going to let myself get into trouble. I wanted to use this time to improve myself. Mostly, I just relaxed as time went by. It's hard to get anything done at a camp.

Time went by fast. I was released into the arms of my parents, who drove a thousand miles to pick me up.

To be honest with you, I didn't want to leave the camp. I had everything I wanted there, except a girlfriend.

This experience brought me closer to my parents. They were always there for me.

I moved in with my parents to start my house arrest. The probation officer wanted me to wear an ankle bracelet. My mother told him that my co-defendants didn't have to wear an ankle bracelet and asked if I could avoid it. (This wasn't exactly the truth. One of my co-defendants served her home confinement in another jurisdiction and had to wear an ankle bracelet.) The probation officer told us not to worry about it.

My parents lived in a small town and the economy was booming. This was fortunate for me, because it was easy to get a job.

My first goal was to get a job. My probation officer seemed like he didn't care if I worked or not.

I started by applying to work at a temporary employment agency. I told the interviewer that I had a criminal record and was currently on house arrest. I always believed honesty was the best policy. I received numerous assignments from this agency. Looking back, I'm not sure being completely honest about my background was the right approach. Many employers don't do background checks, because of the cost. Also, even if a background check had been done, I do not believe my criminal record would have shown up. I paid to do a background check on myself and nothing showed up. It also helps that I have a common first and last name.

Get Off Probation

Millions and millions of Americans have criminal records and most of these people work fulltime. Life goes on and eventually gets better.

I could have easily gotten a job working in construction. It's hard and dangerous work. On the other hand, the money was good.

I worked at a series of temporary jobs. I was just happy to be working. I liked working a lot more than just staying home all day.

My first job was cleaning equipment at a factory. I used dangerous chemicals. There was a revolving door at this company. We had to work twelve hour shifts. A co-worker and myself were both burned by the chemicals, after being on the job for less than a month. I was grateful to be out of there. (I wasn't surprised at all when this company went out of business. Many of the employees would disappear at the beginning of their shift and would reappear when it was time to go home.) I definitely felt like a fish out of water.

I also did backbreaking landscaping work at the local college I had attended ten years earlier. My boss proudly displayed a master's degree from a questionable university in his office. This job paid absolutely nothing. I earned less than I had earned as a high school student. The college had a large endowment for a community college. I was offered a fulltime job as a janitor for a slightly better wage and turned it down.

My self-esteem completely disappeared. I avoided my friends from high school. "You're a complete loser" was constantly in my thoughts. Day and night I felt like a loser.

The temp agency helped me get another backbreaking job stocking soft drinks. I drove from store to store and stocked soft drinks. Again, I was paid virtually nothing. The work was just exhausting. I worked ten or eleven hours and then I went home and just fell asleep. I was also happy when this assignment ended. I believe the company didn't want to keep me because of my criminal record.

A manager at a grocery store offered me a job as a grocery clerk. I took the job because I needed the money. It's good to stay busy. The work was exhausting.

My little sister noticed that I went to the bathroom frequently and constantly drank water and soft drinks. She thought I had diabetes and tested my blood sugar. My blood sugar was through the roof.

My parents drove me to the emergency room. The nurses couldn't believe that I could still walk with such a high blood sugar level. I stayed in the hospital for three days as my blood sugar was brought down. I received excellent medical care.

Being diagnosed with a chronic disease was an eye opener. I changed my life completely. I began exercising more and was more careful about what I ate. I switched to Coke Zero.

The hospital bill was over ten thousand dollars. I couldn't afford to pay it. The hospital agreed to write off most of this amount, but I couldn't even afford to pay the smaller amount.

The drugs I was given made my stomach upset. I've always been reluctant to take any prescriptions.

I quit my job at the grocery store to spend all of my time trying to improve my health. (I enjoyed this job, but quitting was the right decision at the time.) My boss was nice and offered me a job in the office.

I concentrated on taking care of my health and completing my degree. I decided that I didn't need to take any medicine for my condition, because I could manage everything by exercising and watching my diet. I tried this for three months. It was a complete failure. My doctor was furious. Eventually, I realized that I needed to be on the medicine that my doctor had prescribed.

I had a good relationship with my probation officer. He lived in a town that was 80 miles from my parents' house. He visited a few times.

House arrest was okay. In the beginning I was careful to make sure that I was home when I was suppose to be home and followed my curfew. Then I realized that nobody was watching and I could do whatever I wanted to do. I was given permission to travel out of state when it was necessary to complete assignments for my classes. I also was allowed to drive a Uhaul out of state to pick up my belongings from storage.

Get Off Probation

I completed my monthly paperwork and mailed it to my probation officer on time at the end of each month.

I also paid off all of my fines, which were only a few thousand dollars. This impressed everyone. I believe it's very rare for most felons to pay off their fines. In prison, I had friends who were rich and did everything they could to dodge even the smallest fines. I know guys who would get a divorce and give everything to their ex-wives to avoid paying the government a penny. Paying off my fines was a good idea.

I also completed my degree. Again, it's rare for a person on house arrest to complete a degree. I impressed my probation officer and the judge again.

Several months after completing my house arrest, I asked my probation officer what he would think if I asked the judge to get off probation early. He told me that he wouldn't have any objections to my request. Next, I wrote the request and submitted it to the judge, the prosecutor's office and my probation officer.

A Miracle happened. A few weeks later I received a letter from the court granting my motion to terminate my probation. Life was good. I was ready to start my life again.

I was free again and I never planned to get into trouble again.

I loaded my belongings into my car and moved to a large city. The story of my life is still being written. I'm ten times better now than I was when I was going through my criminal case. My life keeps getting better.

"I'm a big believer in the fact that life is about preparation, preparation, preparation."

Johnny Cochran
Criminal Defense Attorney

Chapter Three

Let's Get Started!

This chapter is to help you to complete a preliminary investigation to evaluate your chances of getting off probation early. There's more to getting off probation early than just submitting a motion to the court.

Step One: Determine if you are a good candidate for early termination of probation. (Don't worry if you haven't been perfect during your time on probation. I wasn't perfect and I was able to get off probation early.)

Think about the following as it applies to your situation:

- Have you been on probation for at least a year or have you completed half of your probation? (Generally, you should complete at least half of your probation before asking to be released from probation early.)
- Have you passed all drug tests while you have been on probation?
- Do you have a good relationship with your probation officer?
- Do you currently have a job?
- Are you going to school and making progress towards a GED, degree or a certificate? (Judges are highly educated and place a high value on education.)

- Do you make monthly payments towards your court ordered fines and are you current on your payments? (Best case scenario is to pay your fines off completely.)
- Do you make monthly payments towards court ordered restitution? (Best case scenario is to pay your restitution off completely.)
- Have you stayed out of trouble the entire time you have been on probation?
- Are you in substantial compliance with the terms of your probation?
- Do you do any volunteer work that would put you in a favorable light with the judge?
- Have you cooperated with the authorities or offered to cooperate with the authorities on your case?
- Are there members of the community who will write letters supporting your attempts to get off probation early?
- Are there any other compelling reasons for your probation to be terminated early?

Step Two: Consider other reasons to terminate probation early:

Examples of Reasons for Probation to be Terminated Early:

- I have to frequently take my mother to a neighboring state for treatment and I must ask my probation officer for permission.
- I've been offered a job that involves frequent traveling. I can only accept this job if I am not on probation.
- My good behavior while on probation demonstrates my probation should be terminated early in the interest of justice.
- I want to relocate to another state because the unemployment rate where I currently live is very high. It would be a lot easier for me to start a new life in a new city if I'm off probation.

Step Three: Be completely honest with yourself.

Make your list of reasons why the judge should consider you a good candidate for early termination of probation.

Step Four: Now think of reasons why your request for early termination of probation may be denied.

Reasons Your Request May be Denied

- Frequently failing drug tests.
- Behind on court ordered fines to the court.
- Having a poor relationship with your probation officer.
- Behind on court ordered restitution payments.
- Not submitting your monthly paperwork to your probation officer on time.
- Not having a job or frequently changing jobs. (This may be out of your control, if you live in a city with high unemployment.)
- Not going to court ordered treatment such as AA or NA meetings.
- Getting into any trouble whatsoever with law enforcement when you are on probation.
- Not having a good relationship with your probation officer.
  Make an effort to have a good relationship with your probation officer.
- Not substantially complying with the terms of your probation. (You want to show the court that you are a rule follower.)
- Not being on probation for at least a year or completing half of your time on probation. It's even better if you've completed half of your probation sentence. (You can only ask for termination of your probation once you have been on probation for a while. You can't ask for termination of your probation if you've been on probation for only a short-time.)
- You were convicted of a serious crime. (Generally, the more serious the crime the harder it is to get off probation early.)
- Your case was high profile. (This basically means it was a big news story in your community.)

- Your motion did not clearly show how it would benefit the community if your probation was terminated early.

Step Five: Look at both of your lists.

Try to put yourself in your probation officer's position. Most probation officers are drowning in work and for the most part would like to have a lower caseload. This is true, but your file has to support a justification for early termination of your probation.

Do you think your probation officer would support you in your effort to terminate your probation early. Why or why not? You have to be honest with yourself.

Step Six: Consult with your close friends and family members.

Ask people you respect to examine both lists and for their input. Speak frankly with these individuals about your chances of getting off probation early. Ask these people if they can think of any other reasons to justify early termination of your probation.

It's always a good idea to consult with an attorney on legal matters.

Go to the next step if you believe you have a strong argument to justify terminating your probation early.

If you think you have a weak case, think about what you can do in the future to improve your chances of having your probation terminated early.

Step Seven: Consult with your Probation Officer.

Consult with your probation officer in person if this is possible. (My probation officer lived a hundred miles away from my home and I rarely saw him. I had to call him on the phone.)

Briefly explain to your probation officer why you believe you are a good candidate for early termination of your probation.

Directly ask your probation officer if he or she would support you in getting off probation early. If your probation officer says "yes" this is great. If your probation officer says "no" ask him or her what you can do in the future to get their support on this issue.

Step Eight: Determine who does the paperwork?

Ask your probation officer if he needs to do the paperwork to terminate your probation early or if you should just file a motion with the court. Sometimes probation officers do the paperwork to terminate an individual's probation early. Usually, the individual makes a motion with the court and the judge in the case makes the final determination. Many times the judge sides with the probation officer's recommendation and the recommendation from the prosecutor's office.

(The following states have specific forms you must use to ask the court to terminate probation early: Alaska, Connecticut, Florida, Michigan, North Carolina and Wisconsin. Links to these forms are provided in the Appendix listed under the name of each state.)

Step Nine: (Optional) Contact the prosecutor's office and ask if they would oppose your motion to terminate your probation early. I only recommend contacting the prosecutor's office because it looks good if the prosecutor doesn't oppose your motion. It's also likely the prosecutor's office won't be able to tell you how they would respond to your request.

"Justice in the life and conduct of the state is possible only as first it resides in the hearts and souls of the citizens."

Plato
Philosopher

Chapter Four

Getting Off Probation
Dos and Don'ts

Dos:

- Try your best to have a good relationship with your probation officer. (Remember as long as your on probation, this person has an enormous amount of power over your life.)

- Pay your fines and court ordered restitution. This will impress the court.

- Comply with all terms of your probation. (If you make a mistake, try not to make the same mistake in the future.)

- Become a contributing member of society. This will make you stand out from the crowd. Get a job or go back to school to earn your GED, degree or learn a new trade.

Get Off Probation

- Make a list of reasons why you should be released from probation early. Speak with your friends and family for their input.

- Ask your probation officer if he or she would support your effort to get off probation early. Next, speak with the prosecutor in your case. If either of these individuals opposes your efforts to get off probation early, ask them what you can do in the future to get their support.

- Write your motion. Tell the complete truth. Judges have a gut instinct for spotting the truth. Have a friend proofread your motion. Use MS Word to check the spelling and grammar.

- Writing should be clear, concise and easy to understand. Avoid using ten-dollar words.

- Follow the court rules to properly format and serve your motion to terminate probation early.

- Speak with the court clerk if you have any questions about how to format or serve your motion.

- Consider hiring a lawyer or a paralegal to help you. Interview a minimum of three attorneys before you make your decision. Hire an attorney who practices in the jurisdiction you were convicted in. Try to negotiate a flat fee for the attorney to write and present your motion to the court.

- Make sure you sign your motion and all correspondence sent to the court.

- Send your motion to the court, probation officer and the prosecutor's officer. Follow the court rules to send your motion.

- Schedule a date with the court to hear your motion. (You'll have to speak with the judge's clerk to find out if you need to schedule a hearing. Many times judges will make a decision without having a hearing. This is especially true if neither party opposes the motion.)

- Take a close friend or a family member with you to your court hearing.

- Accept what you cannot change in your life. Put all of your energy into changing for the better what you are able to change.

- Look at the Appendix to get the state or federal statute that gives judges the authority to release defendants from probation early and other state / federal resources.

Don'ts

- Don't do anything to make your probation officer angry. As long as you're on probation, this person has the power to help or destroy you.

- Don't ignore your fines or court ordered restitution. Pay whatever you can afford towards your fines and restitution.

- Don't ignore the terms of your probation. You have to prove that you are a good person to the court and this is done by complying with the terms of your probation.

- Don't get discouraged. If either your probation officer or the prosecutor are against you getting off probation early, ask them what you can do in the future to get their support.

- Don't put anything in your motion that could offend or possibly offend the judge, prosecutor or your probation officer.

- Don't worry if you can't comply with all of the terms of your probation because of circumstances out of your control. (For example, it's not your fault if you can't get a job because you live in a city with high unemployment.)

- Don't give up on yourself. If you make a mistake, learn from the mistake and don't make the same mistake twice.

- Once you've written and submitted your motion, don't worry about it. It's out of your hands. You tried your best, now it's up to the court to make the final determination.

"I find that the harder I work the more luck I seem to have."

Thomas Jefferson
3rd President of the United States
Principal author of the Declaration of Independence

Chapter Five

Making Your Request

Before you do anything, first, contact your probation officer and ask him if he would support your idea to ask the judge for early termination of probation. If your probation officer has any objections whatsoever, I would delay making the request. Judges place a high value on the recommendation of probation officers.

Proceed drafting your request if your probation officer is supportive of the idea.

If your probation officer would oppose your request to getting off probation early, you need to find out under what circumstances he would be supportive of this idea. (The vast majority of probation officers handle a heavy caseload and under the right circumstances, they would be happy to have one less person to supervise.)

Keep in mind your chances of getting off probation early depend on a variety of factors. Among the factors that influence your chances are: 1. the crime you were convicted of, 2. payment of fines, 3. restitution was paid, 4. behavior in custody and on probation, 5. fulfilling community service requirements, 6. the jurisdiction you live in, 7. your probation officer and the presiding judge.

Get Off Probation

It's easier to get off probation early in some communities than others. Some judges and probation officers are more progressive than others and are more likely to grant this request from an offender who can demonstrate that they deserve a second chance. Other judges and probation officers believe that offenders should serve their complete sentences, regardless of mitigating circumstances.

The judge in my case told my co-defendant that her request for early termination of probation was the first one she had received. She had been a judge for many years. She indicated that she would have granted more requests to other defendants, but they need to make the request.

You have to be honest with yourself. If you were convicted of a heinous crime or a high profile crime, this will be difficult to overcome.

Your time is valuable. I wouldn't even make the request, unless you have a reasonable expectation that your request to terminate probation early will be granted. Also, you run the risk of making the judge angry if you request that your probation be terminated early, when there's no chance that even the most liberal judge in the country would rule in your favor. (The judge in your case has complete power over you and you sure don't want to make him or her angry. You can't win a fight with a judge.)

Have realistic expectations. Speak with your friends and family and ask them if they think that you have a chance of getting off probation early. For the most part, have you complied fully with the terms of your probation? Are you doing everything you can to be a productive member of society?

I believe I was able to get off probation early because I paid my fines in full, made full restitution to the government, had a good relationship with my probation officer, was working towards a degree and complied with the terms of my probation. I paid off my fines 4 years early. (While on probation, I was diagnosed with a life altering disease and because of this I quit my job. I had been working at a dead-end job.) Quitting my job allowed me to concentrate on completing my degree in a timely manner. Judges go to work everyday and believe everyone should have a job. Judges want to see defendants who are working and paying taxes. That's a fact.

Get Off Probation

When I was in prison, the other inmates I met did everything they could to avoid paying restitution to their victims and paying anything on their fines. I've only met one other person who made complete restitution and paid his fines in full. Many of the people at the prison camp I was at were convicted of white collar crimes and for the most part, these people had a lot of money. Even the guys with millions and millions of dollars would pay only the bare minimum towards their fines each month and restitution. I think the bare minimum was $5 a month. They would also get "sham" divorces from their wives and transfer all of their assets to their wives.

Was I foolish for making full restitution to the government and paying my fines off early? No, this was one of the best decisions I've made in my life.

I'm convinced that the judge gave me a light sentence to begin with, partially because I had made full restitution before I was to be sentenced. This rarely happens. I stood out. I was looking at up to twenty-years and I only received a relatively short time in prison, house arrest and probation. The prosecutor in my case didn't even come to court for my sentencing. The attorney sent in her place didn't say anything before I was sentenced.

Fast forward a year and a half. The judge in my case granted my motion to terminate probation early. I honestly believe she was impressed by the fact that I had made full restitution and had paid my fines off early. My fines were a few thousand dollars. Even under the best of circumstances, being on probation is difficult. I can remember once I didn't take a trip out of state to visit my father because I wasn't able to get permission from my probation officer. There's nothing good about being on probation.

The judge gave me a break because I didn't thumb my nose at the system. I did the opposite. I went out of my way to follow the rules.

At the very least, you should be current on payments towards your fines and restitution. By making timely payments towards your restitution and fines, you will stand out. The system wants to reward people who follow the rules and do not try to shirk their legal responsibilities.

I was able to get off probation two years early, because I followed the rules and paid off my fines and restitution. You're only free once you are off probation. I always maintained a good relationship with my probation officers. But being on probation is stressful. In the back of my mind, I was always worried that I would end up back in jail.

"A jury consists of twelve persons chosen to decide who has the better lawyer."

Robert Frost
American Poet

Chapter Six

Parts of a Motion

A legal motion is just a request to the court to make a decision related to a case. I labeled the parts of a motion asking the court to terminate a defendant's probation early. All Motions to terminate probation early contain the same elements.

Make an effort to format your motion correctly. The court clerk can reject your motion if the format is incorrect. Format includes the page layout, font size, font type and spacing used in your motion. The easiest way to do this is to copy the format of other court documents in your case. You can also look at the court rules on the court's website or ask the court clerk.

J Jones (A: Name of individual filing motion and contact info.)
111 Main Street
City, State, ZIP Code
Phone Number: (555)555-1212
jxxjones@yahoo.com

J Jones, IN PRO PER (B: Name of individual filing motion.)

(C: Name of the Court and it's location.)
IN THE UNITED STATES DISTRICT COURT

DISTRICT OF XXXX

UNITED STATES OF AMERICA,	) Case No.: CR-XX-XXX-XX-XXX-XXX
	)
Plaintiff,	) DEFENDANT'S MOTION TO TERMINATE PROBATION
	) (D: Name of Defendant's Motion.)
vs.	)
	)
J JONES,	)
	)
Defendant	)

COMES NOW the Defendant, representing myself, who respectfully requests that this Honorable Court terminate my probation pursuant to Rule 32.1 (b) of the Federal Rules of Criminal Procedure and 18 U.S.C. §3564(c). (E: Specific law that gives the court the power to terminate my probation early.) In support of this Motion, I state:

    1.   On XXXX XX, XXXX, I entered a plea of guilty

            to one count of fraud in violation of 18

U.S.C. §1347, a Class X felony. (F: States
the facts of my case.)

2.   I was sentenced on XXXX XX, XXXX to XX months
at a Federal Prison Camp, XX months house
arrest, three years of probation and a $X,XXX
fine and placed under the supervision of the
U.S. Probation Office for the United States
District Court for the District of XXXX. (G:
States the Sentence I was given.)

3.   The statute governing early termination of
probation, 18 U.S.C. §3564(c) provides in
pertinent part that the court may terminate a
term of probation at any time after the
expiration of one year of probation in the
case of a felony if it is satisfied that such
action is warranted by the conduct of the
defendant and the interest of justice. (H:
Specific law that allows the court to
terminate probation early.)

4.   In XXX XXXX, I paid off my $X,XXX fine. (I:
First reason I should be granted early
release of probation.)

5.   While on probation I attended XXXXXX
University and will graduate this XXXX XXXX

with a Degree in XXXXXX. I maintained a X.X grade point average. (J: Second reason I should be granted early release of probation.)

6.   I spoke with Mr. Michael XXXX, my Probation Officer. He reviewed my file, verified that I had paid my fine in full and stated that he did not oppose early termination of my probation. (K: I inform the court that I spoke with my probation officer on this matter.)

7.   Ms. Julia XXXX, the Assistant U.S. Attorney on my case, is no longer employed by the U.S. Attorney's Office. I called the U.S. Attorney's Office to obtain the name of the attorney assigned to my case and I was told that my probation officer would have this information. On XXX XX,XXXX Mr. Michael XXXX contacted the U.S. Attorney's Office to obtain the name of the attorney assigned to my case and was told the U.S. Attorney's Office did not have any records related to my case. (I am sending a copy of my Notice of Orders and Judgment to the U.S. Attorney's

Office with this motion.) (L: I inform the court that I attempted to speak with the prosecutor's office on my motion.)

8.   I have been on probation since XXX X, XXXX, and have proven that I meet the criterion based on my good conduct for early termination of my probation under 18 U.S.C. §3564(c). (M: I re-emphasize that I meet the requirements to be released from probation early and the specific law.)

WHEREFORE, I respectfully request that, in the interest of justice, the Court grant my motion for early termination of probation pursuant to 18 U.S.C. §3564(c) and Rule 32.1(b). (N: I make my request to be released from probation to the Court.)

DATED: XXX XX, XXXX. (O: Date motion was made.)

                                        J Jones (P: Signature.)

                            _____
                                        J Jones
                                        In Pro Per

                            (Q: Certificate of Service: List of all parties that will receive a copy of the motion. This includes the Clerk of the Court, the prosecuting attorney and your probation officer.)

Original of the foregoing
Motion
Mailed / hand-delivered
this XX
day of XXX, XXXX, to:

Clerk of Court
XXXX U.S. Courthouse
Suite XXXX
123 West Main Street
Any City, XX XXXXX

Copy of the foregoing
Motion
Mailed / hand-delivered
this XX
Day of October, XXXX to:

U.S. Attorney
Attn. Mrs. Julia XXXX
123 Oak Avenue, Suite XXX
Any City, XX XXXXX

Mr. Michael XXXX
U.S. Probation Officer
500 Elm Avenue, Suite 123
Any City, XX, XXXXX

By: _George XXXX_ (R:
Signature of person mailing
or hand delivering the
motion.)
  George XXXX

"He who opens a school door closes a prison."

Victor Hugo
French Novelist

Chapter Seven

Must Give Notice

You must notify all of the parties involved in your case after you have scheduled a hearing with the court or you have filed a motion with the court. The notice must be sent to your probation officer and the prosecutor's office. First, speak with the judge's assistant to determine if you need to schedule a hearing on your motion to terminate probation early. (It's possible that the judge will not require a court hearing. Under these circumstances, you still need to give notice to all of the parties involved in your case that you have submitted a motion to terminate probation to the court.)

The notice must be served by an individual who is not personally involved in the case. The individual who serves this notice must be over 18 years old and not involved in the case. Generally, the notice of court hearing can be sent by mail. Using certified mail / return receipt requested is great, because you will have proof that the other party received your notice. (Look at the local court rules for further clarification or ask the court clerk.) Your motion can also be hand delivered to each of the parties.

After serving the Notice of Motion Hearing, the individual who served the motion needs to fill out an affidavit of service.

Schedule your court hearing before you file your Motion to Terminate Probation. By doing this, both your Notice of Hearing and Motion to Terminate Probation can be served at the same time.

Get Off Probation

All of the documents in this book contain an affidavit / certificate of service. It's always at the end of a legal document.

Sample Affidavit / Certificate of Service Language:

```
                         Original of the foregoing Motion
                         Mailed / hand-delivered this XX
                         day of October, XXXX, to:

                         Clerk of Court
                         XXXX U.S. Courthouse
                         Suite XXXX
                         123 West Main Street
                         Any City, XX XXXXX

                         Copy of the foregoing Motion
                         Mailed / hand-delivered this XX
                         Day of October, XXXX to:

                         U.S. Attorney
                         Attn. Mrs. Julia XXXX
                         123 Oak Avenue, Suite XXX
                         Any City, XX XXXXX

                         Mr. Michael XXXX
                         U.S. Probation Officer
                         500 Elm Avenue, Suite 123
                         Any City, XX, XXXXX
                         By: George XXXX
                              George XXXX
```

Get Off Probation

Defendant's Notice of Hearing and Motion to Terminate Probation

J Jones <u>(A: Name of individual filing motion and contact info.)</u>
111 Main Street
City, State, ZIP Code
Phone Number: (555)555-1212
jxxjones@yahoo.com

J Jones, IN PRO PER <u>(B: Name individual filing motion.)</u>

<u>(C: Name of the Court and it's location.)</u>
IN THE UNITED STATES DISTRICT COURT

DISTRICT OF XXXX

UNITED STATES OF AMERICA,	)	Case No.: CR-XX-XXX-XX-XXX-XXX
	)	
Plaintiff,	)	DEFENDANT'S NOTICE OF HEARING
	)	AND MOTION TO TERMINATE
	)	PROBATION
vs.	)	<u>(D: Name of Defendant's</u>
	)	<u>Motion.)</u>
J Jones,	)	DATE: APRIL X, XXXX
	)	TIME: 1:30 PM
	)	<u>(E: Date and time of hearing.)</u>
Defendant		

NOTICE IS HEREBY GIVEN that at the time and place stated above, or as soon thereafter as the matter may be heard, defendant J Jones, will move the court for an order reducing the term of his probation, and to order said probation terminated as of the date of the hearing on this motion.

This motion is made on the grounds that the defendant has substantially met the terms of his probation and is entitled to early release from probation in the interest of justice. This court has the inherent and statutory power and authority under Rule 32.1 (b) of the Federal Rules of

Criminal Procedure and 18 U.S.C. §3564(c). (F: Specific law that gives the court the power to terminate probation.)

This motion is based on this notice of motion, the memorandum of points and authorities filed herewith, the declarations submitted herewith, on the papers and records on file herein, and on such evidence as may be presented at the hearing on this motion.

Dated: XXX XX, XXXX (G: Date motion was made.)

_____*J Jones*_____ (H: Signature.)
J Jones
(I: Certificate of Service: List of all parties that will receive a copy of the motion.)

Original of the foregoing
Motion
Mailed / hand-delivered
this XX
day of October, XXXX, to:

Clerk of Court
XXXX U.S. Courthouse
Suite XXXX
123 West Main Street
Any City, XX XXXXX

Copy of the foregoing
Motion
Mailed / hand-delivered
this XX
Day of October, XXXX to:

U.S. Attorney
Attn. Mrs. Julia XXXX
123 Oak Avenue, Suite XXX
Any City, XX XXXXX

Mr. Michael XXXX
U.S. Probation Officer
500 Elm Avenue, Suite 123
Any City, XX, XXXXX

By: *George XXXX*
(J: Signature of person delivering the motion.)

George XXXX

"If you're walking down the right path and you're willing to keep walking, eventually you'll make progress."

President Barack Obama

Chapter Eight

Hiring a Lawyer

There was a time in my life when I had a very low opinion of lawyers. For a while, I thought attorneys were the lowest of the low, even lower than the individuals who caused the financial crisis.

My opinion changed fast when I lived in a foreign country that wasn't free. The foreign country I lived in had a prime minister, but was in reality controlled by the military. The news media was censored and you could go to jail for a long time for criticizing the leaders. Corruption was everywhere. The police openly took bribes. There was no legal system to speak of. I should say there was a legal system, but there was no justice. Court decisions were based upon who gave the largest bribe to the judges. Corruption destroys a country. In this foreign country, the vast majority of people, including myself, had no rights. Discrimination was open and in your face and you couldn't do anything about it. Employers were free to discriminate based upon age, gender, sexual orientation and skin color. The discrimination made me sick. The rich became richer and the poor became poorer. In this foreign country, only the rich and powerful were protected by the government. The rest of us had no legal recourse whatsoever. Unfortunately, the majority of people do not live in free and democratic societies.

America is a country built on laws. People died to give us the freedom we now take for granted. Lawyers are necessary to insure justice and protect our individual liberties and prevent the government from taking away our rights. America has a lot of lawyers, but these individuals make the USA a better country for everyone to live in. The American legal system isn't perfect, but it's far superior to the legal system in many other countries. I'm grateful for the Constitution and that I was born in the land of the free and the home of the brave.

Speak with your probation officer before you hire an attorney. I believe it would be difficult to get off probation early if your probation officer has any objections.

There are advantages to hiring a lawyer to help you. Hiring an attorney is the best route to writing and submitting your motion to terminate probation to the court. I recommend hiring an attorney if you have the financial resources.

You want to hire a lawyer who has prior experience in criminal defense and practices in the jurisdiction in which you were convicted. Preferably, you want an attorney who specializes in criminal defense.

There are many ways to find an attorney. Ask your friends and family for a recommendation. You can also look in the yellow pages, search on Google or the Martindale Hubbard Directory (http://www.martindale.com). There is no shortage of qualified attorneys in America. (See Chapter 12 Legal Resources.)

Interview at least three attorneys before you make your decision. Trust your gut instincts. You have to be comfortable with the attorney you hire.

During your initial consultation, you need to communicate with each attorney why you are a good candidate to be released from probation early. Bring a list of reasons with you. You have to be completely honest with your attorney about everything.

America is a country built on laws and has become one of the most litigious societies in the history of the world. (I honestly cannot imagine any country, past or present, being more litigious than the United States.) On a per capita basis, America has more attorneys than any other country in the world. The sheer number of attorneys in the marketplace reduces the cost of hiring an attorney. Legal fees vary dramatically across the country.

Try to negotiate a flat rate for the attorney to write and file the motion to terminate probation early. The contract needs to specify what the attorney is expected to do and how much he or she will be paid for their services. (A verbal promise is worthless. The agreement needs to be in writing.)

The big problem with agreeing to pay an hourly rate is that the costs can quickly escalate and you end up owing a lot more than the price you were initially quoted. At the very least you need a written estimate for the legal fees involved in this matter.

The contract should specify that the attorney will draft and file the motion within 30 days. This let's the attorney know that you want this matter taken care of immediately.

Remember, your lawyer works for you. If you are not happy for any reason, you can fire your attorney. Keep in mind, that your attorney would be entitled to keep any fees that had been earned.

If you are not happy with your attorney, immediately communicate your feelings. You can also go to the local bar association and file for fee arbitration dispute. The bar association will hear your complaint and your lawyer's response. They will make a decision based upon this information.

"Failure is not an option. Everyone has to succeed."

Arnold Schwarzenegger
Actor, Politician

Chapter Nine

Drafting the Judge's Order

You may need to write the judge's order on your motion to terminate probation. (This is not common, but I read about it enough times that I wanted to include it.) Contact the judge's assistant and ask if you need to write the judge's order. This would be more common in smaller courts that do not receive adequate funding. (Most likely you will not have to do this in larger, well funded courts. The federal courts are well funded.) You can download judge's orders at www.getoffprobation.com/motion or http://tinyurl.com/getoffprobationfile

Judge's Order Granting Defendant's Motion

SUPERIOR COURT OF THE STATE OF XXX XXXXXX

COUNTY OF XXX

STATE OF XXX XXXXXX,	) Case No.: CR-XX-XXX-XX-XXX-XXX
	)
Plaintiff,	) ORDER
	)
	)
vs.	)
	)
J JONES,	)
	)
Defendant	)

_____

The Court has reviewed defendant's pro se motion to terminate probation, the Government's response and probation department's memorandum.

It is ordered granting defendant's motion.

Dated this _____ day of _____, _____

_____

Jane Doe
XXX XXXXX District Judge

Get Off Probation

Judge's Order Denying Defendant's Motion

SUPERIOR COURT OF THE STATE OF XXX XXXXXX

COUNTY OF XXX

STATE OF XXX XXXXXX,   ) Case No.: CR-XX-XXX-XX-XXX-XXX
)
              Plaintiff,   ) ORDER
)
)
     vs.   )
)
J JONES,   )
)
              Defendant   )

The Court has reviewed defendant's pro se motion to terminate probation, the Government's response and probation department's memorandum.

It is ordered denying defendant's motion.

Dated this _____ day of _____, _____

_____

Jane Doe
XXX XXXXXX District Judge

"If you spend too much time thinking about a thing, you'll never get it done."

Bruce Lee

Chapter Ten

Step by Step

Relax: Don't let the process of writing and filing your motion intimidate you. Just follow each of the steps and try your best. It's not a matter of life or death. If you make a mistake the worst thing that can happen is your motion is rejected and you are free to make corrections and re-file your motion at a later date.

Step One: Look at the Appendix for the state you will be filing your motion in. The notes after each state will tell you if there are specific state forms or other resources that you should use to file your motion to terminate probation early. **(The following states have specific forms you must use to ask the court to terminate probation early: Alaska, Connecticut, Florida, Michigan, North Carolina and Wisconsin. Links to these forms are provided in the Appendix listed under the name of each state.)**

Step Two: Learn the court rules. If you don't look at the court rules, you risk having your motion rejected by the court.

Google the court in which you were convicted and examine the rules online. You can also find the rules in a law library or ask the court clerk if there is any information available to help you learn the rules.

You can find the local court rules at http://www.smartrules.com, http://www.loislaw.com, http://www.fastcase.com, http://law.justia.com, http://www.llrx.com and http://www.law.cornell.edu all provide links to court rules.

(Smartrules, Loislaw and Fastcase all are paid subscription sites, but you may be able to get a free trial subscription to these sites. Overall, the paid subscription sites do a much better job of presenting the court rules in an easy to understand manner. Google the name of the site (Smartrules, Loislaw or Fastcase) and "free trial.") There are a lot of great legal sites on the Internet. We are living in the golden age of information. See Chapter Twelve for additional online resources that provide access to court rules.

You will have to speak with the court clerk if you have any questions about the court rules. Court clerks cannot give legal advice on your case, but they should be able to answer questions related to filing documents with the court. Many courts also have a manual to help defendants who are representing themselves.

It's common for courthouses to also have a law library. The law librarian should be able to give you formatting guidelines and other court rules. A good public library will also have the local courthouse rules in the reference section of the library.

Try to have a good relationship with the court clerk and the judge's assistant. This is necessary, because you most likely will have to ask them for assistance in the future.

Step Three: Schedule a Court Hearing:

Start by contacting the judge's assistant and asking if you need to schedule a hearing on your motion to terminate probation early. It's possible that the judge will consider your motion without a hearing. Judge's have discretion in performing their duties.

Schedule a court hearing on your motion to terminate probation early with the judge who sentenced you. This is done by contacting the court clerk or the judge's assistant. (You may be told that you cannot schedule the hearing until you have filed your motion with the court.) Always be prepared for the unexpected.

Schedule the court hearing four to eight weeks into the future. This will give you plenty of time to file your motion and notify all of the parties involved in your case.

The court clerk will ask for the case number, the name of the motion and the date you want to schedule the hearing for.

Ask the court clerk if you will have to pay a fee to file your motion. You can file a motion to have the fee waived if you are indigent.

Step Four: Formatting Your Motion:

Best Advice: Look at the court rules to determine how to format your motion.

Real Life: Some people don't have the time to learn the ins and outs of formatting their motion. Therefore, they just copy the legal format of their court documents. Other individuals just make up the formatting and submit it to the courts. Worst case scenario, the court clerk may reject your motion if it's not formatted correctly. That's the risk you are taking if you don't look at the court rules. On the other hand, many courts have accepted motions from defendants who have completely ignored formatting rules. (Ted Kaczynski AKA the Unabomber, once submitted a handwritten motion for return of his property in federal court and the motion was accepted.) It's possible the court could reject your motion if it's not formatted properly.

You can also examine the other documents in your case and determine how to properly format your motion. (Following the format of the other court documents in your case is the easiest approach to take.) http://www.smartrules.com, http://www.fastcase.com and http://www.loislaw.com all do a good job of explaining the formatting requirements in plain English and may offer a free trial subscription.

Law librarians and court clerks are both valuable resources. Ask them specifically about the formatting rules for this court. These are common questions and a court clerk or a law librarian should be able to help you.

What you need to pay attention to:

1. Margins

2. Spacing

3. Font

4. Typeface

5. Justification

6. Is pleading paper required? (Pleading paper has numbers.)

Example: The Court Rules for Florida

1. Margins: 1" on all sides.

2. Spacing: Single space all headers, headings, footers, footnotes and extended quotation. Double-space the body of the pleading.

3. Font: Use either 14 point Times New Roman or Courier New 12-point fonts. However, for the redundant or generalized pleadings it is acceptable to use 12-point Times New Roman.

4. Typeface: All material should be presented in ordinary type. Exceptions are italics or underlining citations. Bold typeface Is for you to decide, however it distracts the reader from your pleading.

5. Justification: The body of your pleading can be set to left justification or full justification.

Step Five: Write the Following Documents:

1. Motion to Terminate Probation.

2. Optional: Two orders from the Judge. (Most likely you will not have to write these documents.) The first order granting your request and the second order denying your request. (This is sometimes required at smaller courts, but normally the court prepares the judge's order. You will have to ask the court clerk if you need to write these orders for the judge.) The federal courts are well funded and you will never have to write an order for a federal judge.

3. Notice of Court Hearing, which notifies all of the parties involved of the date, time and location of the hearing on your motion. (Only necessary if the court requires a court hearing on your motion.)

You can download fill in the blank templates of all of these documents at http://www.getoffprobation.com/motion or http://tinyurl.com/getoffprobationfile

Write your motion in the correct format. Look at the court rules or ask the court clerk or a law librarian about formatting rules for the court. (Some courts are lenient to defendants who are representing themselves. Others are strict about the rules.)

Step Six: **Make sure you sign all of the documents**. Use a pen with blue ink to sign all court documents. Court clerks and judges are free to reject legal documents that are not signed.

Step Seven: **Serve Your Motion:**

Warning: You cannot serve your own motion. You will need help serving your motion.

A person who is over the age of eighteen and is not involved in the case has to serve the motion.

You need to get a friend to mail the motion to the following parties: 1. Probation officer and 2. Prosecutor's Office.

Generally, to serve legal documents a person must be eighteen and not personally involved with the case. Therefore, you cannot serve your own motion.

Usually, your motion can be mailed to all of the parties involved. Motions can also be hand delivered in person.

Use certified mail, return receipt requested to mail your motion. The individual who mails the motions to all of the parties should immediately fill out an affidavit or certificate of service.

Certificate of Service: Part One:

All of the legal documents in this book contain a certificate of service at the end of the document.

Best Advice: Get the Certificate or Affidavit of Service that is used in your state.

There are four ways to get the correct Certificate of Service that is used in your state or by the federal courts: 1. Go to the court's website and download it; 2. Google the name of your state or the name of the federal court and the phrase "certificate of service form"; 3. Ask the court clerk where you can get the Certificate of Service that is commonly used in the court; 4. Go to a law library and use a legal forms book to find the correct Certificate of Service. Ask a law librarian if you need any assistant.

Real Life: The Certificate or Affidavit of service just needs to state: 1. The date the motion was sent, 2. Who the motion was sent to and 3. How the motion was delivered to these parties, and 4. Name and signature of the person who sent the motion to all of the parties. (See the sample Certificate of Service below.)

The following site provide affidavits of service for many states: http://www.serve-now.com/resources/legal-forms,

Certificate of Service: Part Two:

The individual who mailed your motion must fill out and sign a "certificate of service" or an "affidavit of service."

A certificate of service states that the motion was in fact sent to all of the parties, the date and how it was sent.

Sample Certificate: (Use the Certificate of Service that is acceptable by the court. Generally, an affidavit of service includes the following information.)

"I certify that a copy hereof has been furnished to (insert names of all individuals who will be sent a copy of the legal documents) by (method of delivery) on (date).

_____
Signature

_____
Name of person who served the legal documents

_____
Address

_____
City, State, Zip code

_____
Phone Number

_____
Email Address

Sample Affidavit / Certificate of Service Language:

```
Original of the foregoing Motion
Mailed / hand-delivered this XX
day of October, XXXX, to:

Clerk of Court
XXXX U.S. Courthouse
Suite XXXX
123 West Main Street
Any City, XX XXXXX

Copy of the foregoing Motion
Mailed / hand-delivered this XX
Day of October, XXXX to:

U.S. Attorney
Attn. Mrs. Julia XXXX
123 Oak Avenue, Suite XXX
Any City, XX XXXXX

Mr. Michael XXXX
U.S. Probation Officer
500 Elm Avenue, Suite 123
Any City, XX, XXXXX

By:

George XXXX
George XXXX
```

Step Eight: **Wait two or three days before going to the courthouse to file your court papers.**

Step Nine: **File with the Court Clerk:**

Best Advice: Go to the courthouse yourself and file your motion with the court clerk by yourself. This will allow the court clerk to tell you immediately if there are any mistakes with the documents you are filing. Expect the unexpected. You may have to pay a fee to file your motion with the court. Also, it's possible the court will tell you that you cannot file your motion. You always have the right to ask the court to terminate your probation early. Just be prepared for anything and don't argue with the clerk. You just want to achieve your objective, which is to file your motion with the court.

Two options:

1. Go to the courthouse and file the motion and certificate of service with the court clerk. Also, give the court clerk a copy of your motion and ask them to stamp it and give it back to you. (Your stamped copy of the motion is your proof that the motion was filed with the court clerk.)

Or:

2. Mail the original motion and a copy of the motion and certificate of service to the court clerk. Enclose a return self-addressed stamped envelope and ask the court clerk to stamp the copy of the motion and return it to you. (Your stamped copy of the motion is your proof that the motion was filed with the court clerk.) **Very Important: Make sure all of the documents have signatures and an Affidavit of Service is included.**

　　　　Clerks may reject motions that are not signed and that do not include an affidavit of service.

Step Ten: A few days before the hearing, confirm with the court clerk that your hearing is still scheduled as planned.

Step Eleven: **The Day of the Hearing:**

Dress like a professional, as if you are going to a job interview. You are judged on the clothes that you wear and how you present yourself. Dress for success.

Arrive early. You don't want to be late for your hearing. Consider staying at a hotel near the courthouse if you live far away. Being late makes you look bad in the eyes of the court. Courthouses, especially in large cities are confusing. It's easy to get lost. Ask a security guard if you need any assistance.

Take into account that you will have to go through a security checkpoint to enter the courthouse. Going to a courthouse is like going to an airport. Security guards are everywhere.

Bring all or your court records.

Take a close friend or relative with you for morale support.

Bring extra copies of your motion, just in case the Judge or another party involved in your case needs a copy.

Step Twelve: Check in with the judge's assistant. The court most likely will be filled with people waiting to argue their motions in front of the judge. You have to check in with the judge's assistant or your case will not be called.

Step Thirteen: Wait until the clerk calls your name.

Stand and address the judge. Speak directly to the judge.

Go out of your way to show your respect for the judge. Refer to the judge as "your honor."

Step Fourteen: State the reasons why the judge should grant your motion to get off probation early. Have a list of talking points that you want to go over when it is your opportunity to address the court. List your reasons and any other activities that put you in a positive light. You want to communicate that it would benefit both you and society overall if you were released from probation early.

Be prepared to answer questions from the judge.

Normally, the judge will rule on the motion immediately. Once the judge has ruled on your motion, ask for a copy of the ruling.

Thank the judge, regardless of how he or she rules on your motion. It's in your best interest to have a good relationship with the judge. Life is filled with surprises. You may be in the courtroom again in the future. Never argue or disrespect a judge.

I also recommend you read attorney Douglas A. Palaschak's AKA The Lawyer Dude's article Motion Writing 101: Fundamentals and Illustrations at http://www.thelawyerdude.com/www.lawyerdud.netfirtms.com/6025.html His website and this article provides a wealth of information on this topic.

Get off Probation

(The following states have specific forms you must use to ask the court to terminate probation early: Alaska, Connecticut, Florida, Michigan, North Carolina and Wisconsin. Links to these forms are provided in the Appendix under the name of each state.)

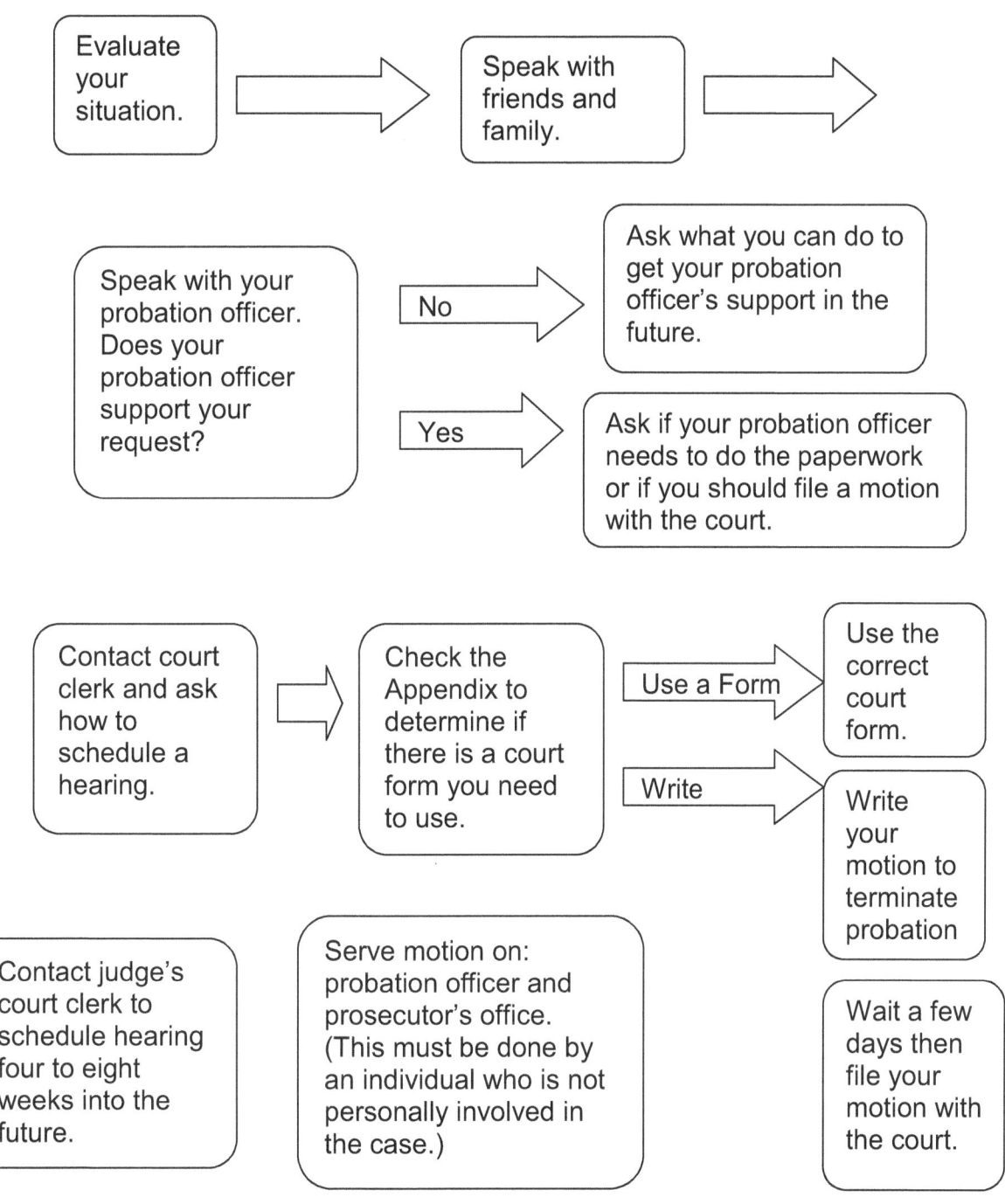

Get Off Probation

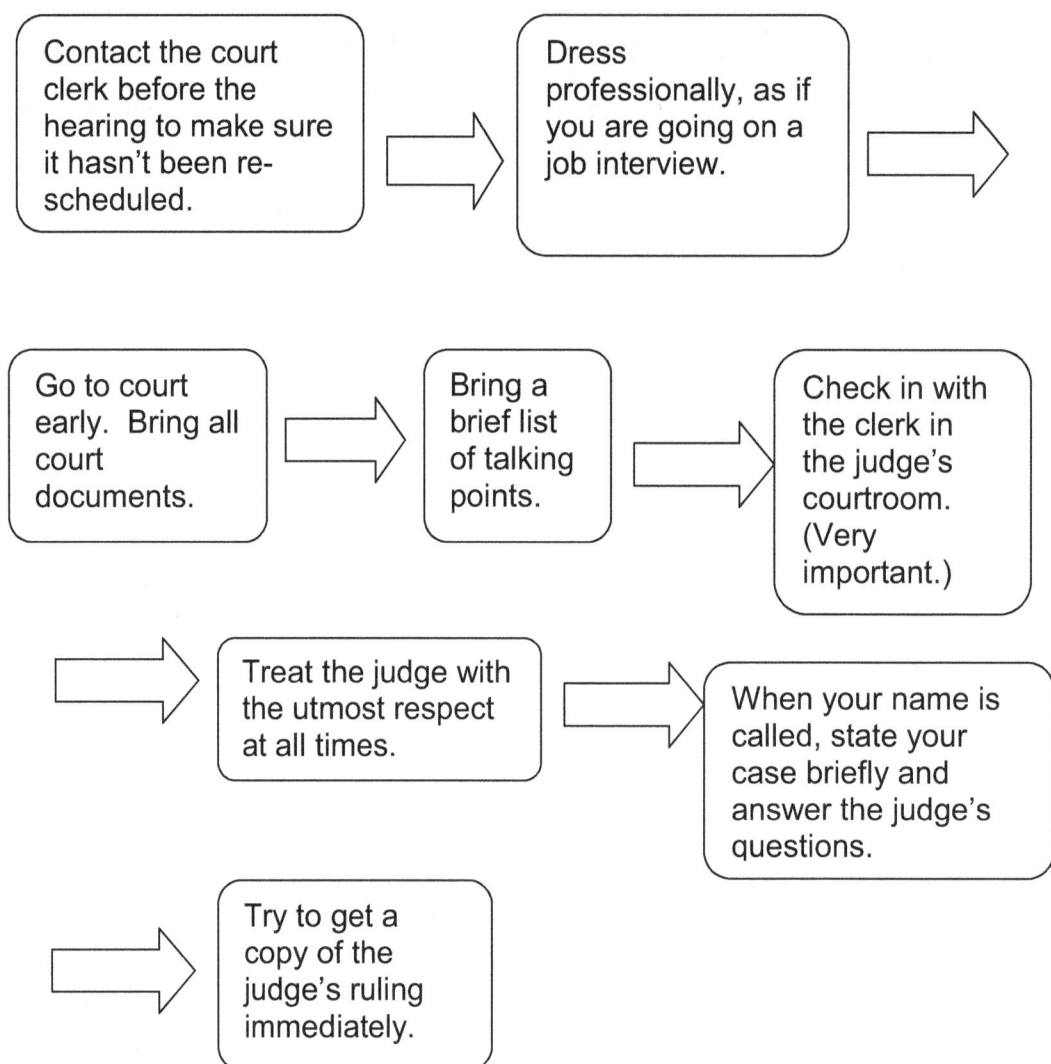

(The following states have specific forms you must use to ask the court to terminate probation early: Alaska, Connecticut, Florida, Michigan, North Carolina and Wisconsin. Links to these forms are provided in the Appendix under the name of each state.)

J Jones
111 Main Street
City, State, ZIP Code
Phone Number: (555)555-1212
jxxjones@yahoo.com

J Jones, IN PRO PER

IN THE UNITED STATES DISTRICT COURT

DISTRICT OF XXXX

UNITED STATES OF AMERICA,	)	Case No.: CR-XX-XXX-XX-XXX-XXX
	)	
Plaintiff,	)	DEFENDANT'S MOTION TO TERMINATE PROBATION
	)	
vs.	)	
	)	
J JONES,	)	
	)	
Defendant	)	

COMES NOW the Defendant, representing myself, who

respectfully requests that this Honorable Court

terminate my probation pursuant to Rule 32.1 (b) of

the Federal Rules of Criminal Procedure and 18 U.S.C.

§3564(c). In support of this Motion, I state:

1.   On XXX XX, XXXX, I entered a plea of guilty to one

count of XXXX fraud in violation of 18 U.S.C. §1347, a

Class X felony.

2. I was sentenced on XXX XX, XXXX to XXX months at a Federal Prison Camp, XXX months house arrest, three years of probation and a $X,XXX fine and placed under the supervision of the U.S. Probation Office for the United States District Court for the District of XXXX.

3. The statute governing early termination of probation, 18 U.S.C. §3564(c) provides in pertinent part that the court may terminate a term of probation at any time after the expiration of one year of probation in the case of a felony if it is satisfied that such action is warranted by the conduct of the defendant and the interest of justice.

4. In XXX XXXX, I paid off my $X,XXX fine.

5. While on probation I attended XXXXXX University and will graduate this XXXX XXXX with a XXXXX Degree in XXXXXXXXXX. I maintained a X.X grade point average.

6. I spoke with Mr. Michael XXXX, my Probation Officer. He reviewed my file, verified that I had paid my fine in full and stated that he did not oppose early termination of my probation.

7. Ms. Julia XXXX, the Assistant U.S. Attorney on my case, is no longer employed by the U.S. Attorney's Office. I called the U.S. Attorney's Office to obtain the name of the attorney assigned to my case and I was

told that my probation officer would have this information. On XXX XX, XXXX Mr. Michael XXXX contacted the U.S. Attorney's Office to obtain the name of the attorney assigned to my case and was told the U.S. Attorney's Office did not have any records related to my case. (I am sending a copy of my Notice of Orders and Judgment to the U.S. Attorney's Office with this motion.)

8.   I have been on probation since XXX X, XXXX, and have proven that I meet the criterion based on my good conduct for early termination of my probation under 18 U.S.C. §3564(c).

WHEREFORE, I respectfully request that, in the interest of justice, the Court grant my motion for early termination of probation pursuant to 18 U.S.C. §3564(c) and Rule 32.1(b).

DATED: XXX XX, XXXX.

J Jones

_____

J Jones
In Pro Per

Original of the foregoing Motion
Mailed / hand-delivered this XX
day of October, XXXX, to:

Clerk of Court
XXXX U.S. Courthouse
Suite XXXX
123 West Main Street
Any City, XX XXXXX

Copy of the foregoing Motion
Mailed / hand-delivered this XX
Day of October, XXXX to:

U.S. Attorney
Attn. Mrs. Julia XXXX
123 Oak Avenue, Suite XXX
Any City, XX XXXXX

Mr. Michael XXXX
U.S. Probation Officer
500 Elm Avenue, Suite 123
Any City, XX, XXXXX

By:

George XXXX

George XXX$\overline{\text{X}}$

Drafting Your Motion & Notice of Hearing

First, gather all of the documents related to your case. Use the following templates to make a draft of your Motion and Notice of Hearing. I recommend that you type both of these documents. (Courts may accept a hand written motion, but you are taking a risk that your motion will be rejected.) Have a friend proofread your motion. You want your motion to look good. Download templates at http://www.getoffprobation.com/motion or http://tinyurl.com/getoffprobationfile

Information Will Need:

1. The name and address of the court.
2. The case number.
3. The state or federal law that gives the judge authority to release you from probation early. (These laws are listed in the Appendix.)
4. The date you were sentenced.
5. The specific sentence and fine.
6. Details of payments you have made towards your fine and restitution.
7. Specific reasons the court should release you from probation early.

Notice of Hearing Tips:

Contact the judge's assistant and ask it you need to schedule a hearing. See Chapter Seven: Must Give Notice for more information.

Formatting Tips:

Formatting consists of page layout, margins, font, font size and spacing. The easiest way to properly format these documents is to copy the format of other legal documents in your case. (You should have copies of all of the documents in your case. Your former attorney or the courthouse can provide you with documents related to your case for a fee.)

Try to format your motion correctly, but don't obsess about it. Keep the formatting consistent. The worst thing that can happen is that your motion is rejected and you can resubmit it later. Type your motion and try your best to make it look good. See Chapter 12: Legal Resources to find websites that link to court rules. http://www.smartrules.com, http://www.fastcase.com and http://www.loislaw.com all do a good job of explaining the court rules. All of these require a paid subscription, but may offer a free trial subscription.

_____ (insert name of individual writing motion)

_____ (insert address)

_____ (insert city, state and zip code)

_____ (insert phone number)

_____ (insert email address)

_____ , IN PRO Per (insert name of person filing the motion)

_____ (insert name of the court)

(insert state name or USA)	Case No._____ (insert case number)
Plaintiff,	DEFENDANT'S NOTICE OF HEARING AND MOTION TO TERMINATE PROBATION
vs.	
(insert Defendant's name)	Date:_____ (insert date of hearing)
Defendant	Time:_____ (insert time of hearing)

NOTICE IS HEREBY GIVEN that at the time and place stated above, or as soon thereafter as the matter may be heard, defendant _____, (insert defendant's name) will move the court for an order reducing the term of his probation, and to order said probation terminated as of the date of the hearing on this motion.

This motion is made on the grounds that the defendant has substantially met the terms of his probation and is entitled to early release from probation in the interest of justice. This court has the inherent and statutory power and authority under

_____ (insert law that allows early termination of probation)

Get Off Probation

Drafting Notice of Hearing

This motion is based on this notice of motion, the memorandum of points and authorities filed herewith, the declarations submitted herewith, on the papers and records on file herein, and on such evidence as may be presented at the hearing on this motion.

Dated:_____ (insert date motion was made)

(signature of individual making the motion) _____

(name of individual making the motion) _____

(circle how motion was delivered) Original of the foregoing Motion Mailed / Hand-delivered this _____ day of _____ _____, to:

Clerk of Court

(insert court name) _____

(insert court address) _____

(insert city, zip code) _____

(circle how motion was delivered) Copy of the foregoing Motion Mailed / Hand Delivered this _____ Day of _____, _____ to:

(insert prosecutor) _____

(address of office) _____

(city, state, zip code) _____

(Prob. Officer's name) _____

(address of office) _____

(city, state, zip code) _____

(signature of person who served motion) _____

(name of person who served motion) _____

Get Off Probation

Drafting Motion to Terminate Probation

_____ (insert name of individual writing motion)

_____ (insert address)

_____ (insert phone number)

_____ (insert email address)

_____, IN PRO Per (insert name of person filing the motion)

_____ (insert name of the court)

_____ (insert state name or USA) Case No._____

Plaintiff,	) DEFENDANT'S MOTION TO
	) TERMINATE PROBATION
vs.	)
	)
_____	)
(insert Defendant's name)	)
	)
Defendant	)

COMES NOW the Defendant, representing myself, who respectfully requests that

this Honorable Court terminate my probation pursuant to _____

(insert statute that gives the court the authority to terminate probation early State

and federal laws are listed in the appendix.) In support of this Motion, I state:

1.   On _____ (insert date you pled or were found guilty), I

_____

(Insert the facts of your case: either you pled guilty or were found guilty by a court

of law) in violation of _____ (insert the law you pled or were found guilty of.) a

Class _____ (insert the class of the felony) felony.

2.   I was sentenced on _____ (insert date you were

sentenced) to _____ (insert your prison sentence) months at a prison,

_____ months house arrest, _____ years of probation and a _____ fine and

Get Off Probation

<u>Drafting Motion to Terminate Probation</u>

placed under the supervision of the _____ (Insert name of

the probation system) Probation Office.

3.   The statute governing early termination of probation _____

(insert state or federal statute that allows the court to terminate probation)

provides in pertinent part that the court may terminate a term of probation at any time

after the expiration of one year of probation in the case of a felony if it is satisfied that

such action is warranted by the conduct of the defendant and the interest of justice.

4. _____

(insert amount you have paid towards your fines: **Example: "On XXX, XXXX I paid**

off my $X,XXX fine." Also, explain how you have complied with all of the terms of

your probation terms.)

5. _____

_____

_____

_____

(insert what you have done while on probation which shows you are being a

productive member of society: **Example: "While on probation I attended XXXXXX**

University and will graduate this XXX, XXXX with a XXXX degree in XXXX. I

maintained a X.X grade point average.")

6. _____

_____

_____

_____

Get Off Probation

Drafting Motion to Terminate Probation

(Optional: insert additional reasons which show you are a productive member of society: **Example: working, volunteering, completing your GED, helping others.**)

7. _____

_____

_____

_____

(Optional: insert additional reasons probation should be terminated early)

8.. I spoke with _____ (insert name of probation officer). He reviewed my file, verified that I had _____ (insert payments you have made towards your fines: **Example: "paid my fine in full."**) and stated that he did not oppose early termination of my probation.

9. _____ (insert name of prosecutor on your case and this person's title: **Example: "Ms. Julia XXXX, the assistant U.S. Attorney on my case)**

_____

_____ (Note if the prosecutor is no longer employed by the prosecutor's office. **Example: "is no longer employed by the U.S. Attorney's Office.)** _____

(insert efforts you have made to contact the prosecutor's office to determine if they have any objections to your motion to terminate probation early: **Example: "I called the U.S. Attorney's Office to obtain the name of the attorney assigned to my case and I was told that my probation officer would have this information. On XXX XX, XXXX Mr. Michael XXXX contacted the U.S. Attorney's Office to obtain the name of the attorney assigned to my case and was told the U.S. Attorney's Office**

did not have any records related to my case. I am sending a copy of my Notice of Orders and Judgment to the U.S. Attorney's Office with this motion.")

10.   I have been on probation since _____, (insert date your probation began) and have proven that I meet the criterion based on my good conduct for early termination of my probation under _____ (insert law that gives the judge the authority to terminate your probation. State and federal laws that allow the courts to terminate probation early are listed in the appendix.)

WHEREFORE, I respectfully request that, in the interest of justice, the Court grant my motion for early termination of probation pursuant to _____ (insert law that gives the judge the authority to terminate your probation. State and federal laws that allow the courts to terminate probation early are listed in the appendix.)

Dated: _____ (insert the date the motion was written)

(signature of individual making the motion)   _____

(name of individual making the motion)   _____

(circle how motion was delivered)   Original of the foregoing Motion Mailed / Hand-delivered this _____ Day of _____ _____, to:

Clerk of Court

(insert court name)   _____

(insert court address)   _____

(insert city, zip code)   _____

(circle how motion was delivered)   Copy of the foregoing Motion Mailed / Hand

Get Off Probation

<u>Drafting Motion to Terminate Probation</u>

Delivered this _____ Day of _____,
_____, to:

(insert prosecutor's name)   _____

(name of office)   _____

(address of office)   _____

(city, state, zip code)   _____

(Prob. Officer's name)   _____

(insert title)   _____

(name of office)   _____

(address of office)   _____

(city, state, zip code)   _____

(signature of person who served motion)   _____

(name of person who served motion)   _____

Get Off Probation

"I will prepare and some day my chance will come."

Abraham Lincoln
16th President of the United States

Chapter Eleven
Closing

Tough Advice from a Friend

We have a lot in common. I was convicted of a crime and served time in prison. I have a criminal record that will most likely be with me for the rest of my life. It's difficult to get a presidential pardon. The criminal record is more difficult to deal with than the actual prison time that I served. I can definitely understand what other ex-offenders are dealing with.

Life isn't fair. Forget about the past because you can't change it, but you are responsible for your own future. Live every day to the fullest.

I want you to overcome the obstacles that ex-offenders face on a daily basis and succeed in your life. Nothing makes me happier than reading about an ex-offender who has worked hard and turned their life around. These are the greatest stories to read. I search for these stories in the morning newspaper. I hope you become a success story.

The best advice I can give you is to stay out of trouble and avoid anything that could get you into trouble. It's not worth getting into trouble again. There are innocent people serving prison sentences because they hung out with the wrong people. Judges give the harshest sentences to repeat offenders. Avoid negative people. Hang out with positive people. They will improve the quality of your life.

Always try your best to be a productive member of society. Take the best job you can find and do your best at it. Having a job, even a bad one is better than being unemployed. As an ex-offender you have to work harder than everyone else. Set reasonable goals for yourself and periodically re-evaluate these goals.

Many states have three strikes and you're out laws. If you get into trouble again, you could go to prison for life. Life is less stressful and more rewarding if you follow the rules. Ex-offenders are held to a higher standard than individuals, who do not have criminal records.

I wish each of you the best of luck.

"There may be more poetry than justice in poetic justice."

George Will
Author, Journalist

Chapter Twelve

Legal Resources

Disclaimer: Warning: The following resources are provided for informational purposes only. The author is not affiliated with and cannot guarantee the accuracy of the information provided from any of the following online resources. Use caution and common sense when accessing third-party websites. The best advice is to always consult an attorney on legal matters.

Attorney Directories:

- **AttorneyFind:**

    Find attorneys in over 70 practice areas.

http://www.attorneyfind.com

- **AVVO:**

    Find the right lawyer based on client reviews, AVVO Ratings, disciplinary history, etc. Search for attorneys near you who specialize in your legal matter.

http://www.avvo.com/find-a-lawyer

- **FindLaw:**

    Comprehensive list of attorneys and their specialty.

http://www.findlaw.com/

- **Lawyer.com:**

  Find a lawyer. Get free legal advice. Over 400,000 lawyers in 200 practice areas listed.

  http://www.lawyer.com/

- **Lawyers.com**

  Claims to be the largest online directory of attorneys and law firms.

  http://www.lawyers.com

- **Martindale-Hubbell Directory:**

  Publisher of the respected *Martindale-Hubbell Directory*.

  http://www.martindale.com/

- **Nolo Press:**

  Online directory of attorneys arranged by specialty and location.

  http://www.nolo.com/

Court Rules:

- **Fastcase:**

  Fastcase puts the whole national law library on your desktop, with online access to cases, statutes, regulations, court rules, and bar publications. Requires a paid subscription. May offer a free trial subscription.

  http://www.fastcase.com

- **LLRX: Law and Technology Resources for Legal Professionals:**

  This site includes links to over 1,400 sources for state and federal court rules, forms and dockets.

  http://www.llrx.com/courtrules

- **Loislaw**

  Loislaw publishes case law, statutory law, constitutions, administrative law, court rules, and other authority for all 50 states and the District of Columbia. Requires a paid subscription. May offer a free trial subscription.

  http://www.loislaw.com

- **Smart Rules:**

  Smart Rules explains the court rules in simple language for many jurisdictions. Smart Rules provides both limited free access and a paid subscription plan. May offer a free trial subscription.

  http://www.smartrules.com

Interesting Websites:

- **Pro Se Way**

  Provides information for pro se litigants trying to navigate the court system.

  http://www.caught.net/prose/prose.htm

- **Pro Se Motion:**

  Well written pro se motion to terminate probation early.

  http://kubby.com/Motion.terminate.html

- **Unabomber's Handwritten Motion:**

  Ted Kaczynski's AKA the Unabomber 150 page handwritten motion asking the court to return his property. This motion was accepted by a federal court.

  http://www.thesmokinggun.com/documents/crime/unabomber-wants-his-stuff-back

- **The Lawyer Dude:**

Created by Douglas Palaschak, who's a California attorney. This website explains the legal process and provides examples of motions. This site was created to help pro se plaintiffs. He also wrote the book *Pro Se Litigation*.

http://www.thelawyerdude.com/

- **National Center for State Courts:**

Provides links for legal self-help and state resources.

http://www.nlsonline.org

Legal Forums:

The Internet has changed the world. Legal forums allow anyone to ask questions. Legal forums are a great place to start, but you need to verify the information you receive with other resources. Don't believe everything you read on the Internet. The paid sites tend to provide higher quality answers from licensed attorneys, who's credentials have been verified.

- **Ask A Lawyer:**

Ask your question at no charge or obligation. The link between consumers, lawyers and the law. Referrals of online inquiries to attorneys in a broad array of practice areas.

http://askalawyer.com/

- **Ask a Lawyer on Call:**

For a fee you can ask lawyers, who's credentials have been verified a legal question. Satisfaction guaranteed. The lawyers don't get paid unless you're satisfied.

http://askalawyeroncall.com/

- **Ask a Lawyer Free:**

Ask a lawyer or an attorney the legal question and get free legal advice, article, news and videos. Thousands of answers from expert attorneys.

http://www.askalawyerfree.com/

- **Ask The Lawyers:**

Is an online legal service devoted to consumers and businesses to find a lawyer in their area to help with their personal legal needs.

http://www.askthelawyers.com/

- **AVVO:**

Alimony to Wrongful termination, AVVO has over 250,000 answers and Legal Guides.

http://www.avvo.com/free-legal-advice

- **Dear Esquire:**

You can ask questions that are answered by a variety of attorneys on this website. It is operated by a law professor and a noted attorney.

http://www.dearesq.com/

- **Expert Law:**

Legal resources you can trust. Free legal help and information. Thousands of answers to legal questions.

http://www.expertlaw.com/forums

- **FindLaw Answers:**

Ask a legal question and let the FindLaw community help you find legal answers and information. Get your law questions answered by members of the FindLaw community.

http://www.findlaw.com/

- **Free Online Legal Advice:**

  Provides a number of ways to get free online legal advice.

  http://www.freeonlinelegaladvice.org/

- **Just Answer Legal:**

  Ask a legal question, name your price and get an answer ASAP!

  http://www.justanswer.com/law

- **Law Guru Answers:**

  "We offer you the knowledge of thousands of attorneys, as well as flexibility and convenience that we know is important to you. From here you can submit either a free question or for a small fee get private confidential advice."

  https://www.lawguru.com/answers/

- **Nolo Press**

  Well known publisher of self-help legal books. Website provides a wealth of information and includes a searchable forum.

  http://www.nolo.com

- **Yahoo! Answers:**

  Yahoo! Answers is a new way to find out and share information. You can ask questions on any topic, get answers from others and share your insights.

  http://answers.yahoo.com/

Legal Resources:

- **All Law:**

  The Internet's premiere law portal.

http://www.alllaw.com/

- **California Courts Self-Help Center**

  Provides a wealth of information on California Courts.

http://www.courtinfo.ca.gov/selfhelp/lowcost/getready.htm

- **Creating California Pleadings**

  Explains in detail how to create California Pleadings.

http://www.saclaw.lib.ca.u/pages/creating-pleadings.aspx

- **FindLaw:**

  Comprehensive legal internet portal. Includes a forum, links to codes, a legal search engine and more.

http://www.findlaw.com/

- **Justia:**

  Provides free case law, codes, regulations and legal information for lawyers, business, students and consumers worldwide.

http://www.justia.com/

- **LawGuru:**

  Search the Internet law library. Search our database of thousands of legal questions and answers in dozens of areas of law from our network of attorneys.

http://www.lawguru.com/

- **LexisNexis:**

  Commonly used by legal professionals. Offers a premium subscription.

http://www.lexis.com

- **LII: Legal Information Institute at Cornell Law School:**

  Primary legal materials and links to a wide array of US and international legal reference websites. From Cornell Law School.

  http://www.law.cornell.edu/

- **LLRX: Law and technology resources for legal professionals.**

  Articles, court rules and resources relating to legal practice, research, and law firm management.

  http://www.llrx.com/

- **MegaLaw:**

  The legal World Wide Web with LawBot the legal search engine, cases, codes, forms and more.

  http://www.megalaw.com/

- **Westlaw:**

  Westlaw is one of the primary online legal research services for lawyers.

  http://www.westlaw.com (premium site)

State & Federal Statutes:

http://topics.law.cornell.edu

http://codes.lp.findlaw.com

http://www.fastcase.com/   (premium, may offer trial subscription.)

http://www.gpoaccess.gov/cfr/   Code of Federal Regulations

http://law.justia.com/

http://www.loislaw.com/   (premium, may offer trial subscription.)

http://www.megalaw.com/states.php

http://www.michie.com/

"If you want to know who your friends are, get yourself a jail sentence."

Charles Bukowski
American Novelist

Freedom

Appendix

State & Federal Law

(The following states have specific forms you must use to ask the court to terminate probation early: Alaska, Connecticut, Florida, Michigan, North Carolina and Wisconsin. Links to these forms are provided in the Appendix under the name of each state.)

Generally, the premium sites are easier to navigate and the information is easier to understand. (Premium sites are websites that require a paid subscription.) If you cannot find a "free trial subscription" offer on a premium website, Google the name of the premium site and "free trial" to find links to free trial subscriptions offers.

The following websites are provided for informational purposes only. The author is not affiliated with any of these websites. Use caution when accessing third party websites.

Court Rules:

http://www.fastcase.com (Paid subscription, may offer free trial subscription.)

http://www.law.cornell.edu/topics/court_rules.html

http://law.nd.edu/library-and-technology/find/state-court-rules/

http://www.llrx.com/courtrules

http://www.loislaw.com (Paid subscription, may offer free trial subscription.)

http://www.megalaw.com

http://www.smartrules.com (Paid subscription, may offer free trial subscription.)

State and Federal Statutes:

http://www.justia.com

http://www.fastcase.com (Paid subscription, may offer free trial subscription.)

http://www.findlaw.com

http://www.law.cornell.edu/states/listing.html

http://www.law.onecle.com

http://www.lawyers.com

http://www.loislaw.com (Paid subscription, may offer free trial subscription.)

http://www.megalaw.com

http://www.michie.com

http://www.nolo.com

http://www.whpgs.org/

Alabama:

Alabama Criminal Code: Title 15: Criminal Procedure, Chapter 22: Pardons,

Paroles and probation, Section 54 (b):

Code of Alabama: Section 15-22-54(b):

(b) The court granting probation may, upon the recommendation of the officer supervising the probationer, terminate all authority and supervision over the probationer prior to the declared date of completion of probation upon showing a continued satisfactory compliance with the conditions of probation over a sufficient portion of the period of the probation.

Source: http://www.legislature.state.al.us/CodeofAlabama/1975/coatoc.htm

Alabama Judicial System: **http://www.judicial.alabama**.gov

Alaska:

Alaska Statutes: Title 12 Code of Criminal Procedure, Chapter 55 Sentencing and Probation, Section 85 Suspending Imposition of Sentence.

Alaska Statutes 12.55.085. Suspending Imposition of Sentence.

 (d) The court may at any time during the period of probation revoke or modify its order of suspension of imposition of sentence. It may at any time, when the ends of justice will be served, and when the good conduct and reform of the person held on probation warrant it, terminate the period of probation and discharge the person held. If the court has not revoked the order of probation and pronounced sentence, the defendant shall, at the end of the term of probation, be discharged by the court.

(e) Upon the discharge by the court without imposition of sentence, the court may set aside the conviction and issue to the person a certificate to that effect.

(f) The court may not suspend the imposition of sentence of a person who

(1) is convicted of a violation of AS <u>11.41.100</u> - <u>11.41.220</u>, <u>11.41.260</u> - <u>11.41.320</u>, <u>11.41.410</u> - <u>11.41.530</u>, or AS <u>11.46.400</u> ;

(2) uses a firearm in the commission of the offense for which the person is convicted; or

(3) is convicted of a violation of AS <u>11.41.230</u> - <u>11.41.250</u> or a felony and the person has one or more prior convictions for a misdemeanor violation of AS <u>11.41</u> or for a felony or for a violation of a law in this or another jurisdiction having substantially similar elements to an offense defined as a misdemeanor in AS <u>11.41</u> or as a felony in this state; for the purposes of this paragraph, a person shall be considered to have a prior conviction even if that conviction has been set aside under (e) of this section or under the equivalent provision of the laws of another jurisdiction.

*Must use Alaska Form CR-500 to make request to terminate probation early.

<u>http://www.courts.alaska.gov/forms/adm-510.pdf</u> **(I was not able to find a link to this form online. This form should be available at either the courthouse or in a criminal form book at a law library.)**

Site: <u>http://www.legis.state.ak.us</u>

Alaska Court System: <u>http://www.courts.alaska.gov/</u>

Arizona:

Arizona Code: Title 13 Criminal Code: Arizona Revised Statutes §13-901 Probation:

E. The court, on its own initiative or on application of the probationer, after notice and an opportunity to be heard for the prosecuting attorney and, on request, the victim, may terminate the period of probation or intensive probation and discharge the defendant at a time earlier than that originally imposed if in the court's opinion the ends of justice will be served and if the conduct of the defendant on probation warrants it.

Source: http://law.justia.com/arizona/codes/title13/00901.html

Arizona Judicial Branch: http://www.**azcourts.gov**

Arkansas:

Ark. Code 5-4-306 Time period generally - Modification

(a) (1) If a court suspends imposition of sentence on a defendant or places him or her on probation, the period of suspension or probation shall be for a definite period of time not to exceed the maximum jail or prison sentence allowable for the offense charged.

(2) The court may discharge the defendant at any time.

(b) During a period of suspension or probation, upon the motion of a probation officer or a defendant or upon the court's own motion, a court may:

(1) Modify a condition imposed on the defendant;

(2) Impose an additional condition authorized by Sec. 5-4-303;

(3) Impose an additional fine authorized by Sec. 5-4-201 and 5-4-303; or

(4) Impose a period of confinement authorized by Sec. 5-4-304.

Source: http://www.arkleg.state.ar.us
Arkansas Judiciary: http://courts.state.ar.us/

California:

California Penal Code Section 1203.3:.

(a) The court shall have authority at any time during the term of probation to revoke, modify, or change its order of suspension of imposition or execution of sentence. The court may at any time when the ends of justice will be subserved thereby, and when the good conduct and reform of the person so held on probation shall warrant it, terminate the period of probation, and discharge the person so held.

(b) The exercise of the court's authority in subdivision (a) to revoke, modify, change, or terminate probation is subject to the following:

(1) Before any sentence or term or condition of probation is modified, a hearing shall be held in open court before the judge. The prosecuting attorney shall be given a two-day written notice and an opportunity to be heard on the matter, except that, as to modifying or terminating a protective order in a case involving domestic violence, as defined in Section 6211 of the Family Code, the prosecuting attorney shall be given a five-day written notice and an opportunity to be heard.

(A) If the sentence or term or condition of probation is modified pursuant to this section, the judge shall state the reasons for that modification on the record.

(B) As used in this section, modification of sentence shall include reducing a felony to a misdemeanor.

(2) No order shall be made without written notice first given by the court or the clerk thereof to the proper probation officer of the intention to revoke, modify, or change its order.

(3) In all cases, if the court has not seen fit to revoke the order of probation and impose sentence or pronounce judgment, the defendant shall at the end of the term of probation or any extension thereof, be by the court discharged subject to the provisions of these sections.

(4) The court may modify the time and manner of the term of probation for purposes of measuring the timely payment of restitution obligations or the good conduct and reform of the defendant while on probation. The court shall not modify the dollar amount of the restitution obligations due to the good conduct and reform of the defendant, absent compelling and extraordinary reasons, nor shall the court limit the ability of payees to enforce the obligations in the

manner of judgments in civil actions.

(5) Nothing in this section shall be construed to prohibit the court from modifying the dollar amount of a restitution order pursuant to subdivision (f) of Section 1202.4 at any time during the term of the probation.

(6) The court may limit or terminate a protective order that is a condition of probation in a case involving domestic violence, as defined in Section 6211 of the Family Code. In determining whether to limit or terminate the protective order, the court shall consider if there has been any material change in circumstances since the crime for which the order was issued, and any issue that relates to whether there exists good cause for the change, including, but not limited to, consideration of all of the following:

(A) Whether the probationer has accepted responsibility for the abusive behavior perpetrated against the victim.

(B) Whether the probationer is currently attending and actively participating in counseling sessions.

(C) Whether the probationer has completed parenting counseling, or attended alcoholics or narcotics counseling.

(D) Whether the probationer has moved from the state, or is incarcerated.

(E) Whether the probationer is still cohabiting, or intends to cohabit, with any subject of the order.

(F) Whether the defendant has performed well on probation, including consideration of any progress reports.

(G) Whether the victim desires the change, and if so, the victim's reasons, whether the victim has consulted a victim advocate, and whether the victim has prepared a safety plan and has access to local resources.

(e) This section does not apply to cases covered by Section **1203**.2.

Source: http://law.justia.com/california/codes/2009/pen/1191-1210.5.html

The following link provides a wealth of information for individuals in California:
http://www.courtinfo.ca.gov//selfhelp/lowcost/getready.htm
California Courts: http://www.courtinfo.ca.gov/

Colorado:

Colorado Revised Statute, Title 18 Criminal Code, Article 1.3 Sentencing in Criminal Cases, Part 2 Probation 18-1.3-202 Probationary Power of Court: Colorado Revised Statute: Section 18-1.3-202:

(1) When it appears to the satisfaction of the court that the ends of justice and the best interest of the public, as well as the defendant, will be served thereby, the court may grant the defendant probation for such period and upon such terms and conditions as it deems best. The length of probation shall be subject to the discretion of the court and may exceed the maximum period of incarceration authorized for the classification of the offense of which the defendant is convicted but shall not exceed five years for any misdemeanor or petty offense. If the court chooses to grant the defendant probation, the order placing the defendant on probation shall take effect upon entry and, if any appeal is brought, shall remain in effect pending review by an appellate court unless the court grants a stay of probation pursuant to section 16-4-201, C.R.S. Unless an appeal is filed that raises a claim that probation was granted contrary to the provisions of this title, the trial court shall retain jurisdiction of the case for the purpose of adjudicating complaints filed against the defendant that allege a violation of the terms and conditions of probation. In addition to imposing other conditions, the court has the power to commit the defendant to any jail operated by the county or city and county in which the offense was committed during such time or for such intervals within the period of probation as the court determines. The aggregate length of any such commitment whether continuous or at designated intervals shall not exceed ninety days for a felony, sixty days for a misdemeanor, or ten days for a

petty offense unless it is a part of a work release program pursuant to section 18-1.3-207. That the defendant submit to commitment imposed under this section shall be deemed a condition of probation.

Source: http://www.michie.com/colorado

The following link provides information on Colorado probation:
http://www.courts.state.co.us/Probation/Index.cfm

Colorado Judicial Branch: http://www.courts.state.co.us/

Connecticut:

Connecticut: Connecticut Code, Title 53a Chapter 952 Sections 53a-33 to Sections 53a-34
Connecticut Code, Sec. 53a-33. Termination of probation or conditional discharge. The court or sentencing judge may at any time during the period of probation or conditional discharge, after hearing and for good cause shown, terminate a sentence of probation or conditional discharge before the completion thereof, except a sentence of probation imposed for conviction of a violation of subdivision (2) of section 53-21 of the general statutes in effect prior to October 1, 2000, subdivision (2) of subsection (a) of section 53-21 or section 53a-70, 53a-70a, 53a-70b, 53a-71, 53a-72a or 53a-72b.

 Sec. 53a-34. Unconditional discharge: Criteria; effect. (a) The court may impose a sentence of unconditional discharge in any case where it is authorized to impose a sentence of conditional discharge under section 53a-29, if the court is of the opinion that no proper purpose would be served by imposing any condition upon the defendant's release.

(b) When the court imposes a sentence of unconditional discharge, the defendant shall be released with respect to the conviction for which the sentence is imposed without imprisonment, probation supervision or conditions. A sentence of unconditional discharge is for all purposes a final judgment of conviction.

Source: http://law.justia.com/connecticut/codes/title53a/sec53a-33.html

*Use Connecticut Form JD-CR_59, PROBATION/CONDITIONAL DISCHARGE MOTION JD-CR-59 Rev. 11-06

Available at: http://www.jud2.ct.gov/webforms/forms/cr059.pdf

Connecticut Judicial Branch: http://www.jud.state.ct.us/

Delaware:

Delaware Code, Title 11 – Crimes and Criminal Procedure, Chapter 43 – Sentencing, Probation, Parole and Pardons, Subchapter III – Probation and Sentencing Procedures Section 4333 – Period of probation or suspension of sentence; termination.

Delaware Code: Title 11, Section 4333. Period of probation or suspension of sentence; termination.

(a) The period of probation or suspension of sentence shall be fixed by the court subject to the provisions of this section. Any probation or suspension of sentence may be terminated by the court at any time and upon such termination or upon termination by expiration of the term, an order to this effect shall be entered by the court.

Source: http://law.justia.com/delaware/codes/title11/c043-sc03.html

Delaware Judicial Branch: http://courts.delaware.gov

Federal:

18 U.S. Code, Section 3564 (c): Running of a term of probation

Get Off Probation

a) Commencement.— A term of probation commences on the day that the sentence of probation is imposed, unless otherwise ordered by the court.

(b) Concurrence With Other Sentences.— Multiple terms of probation, whether imposed at the same time or at different times, run concurrently with each other. A term of probation runs concurrently with any Federal, State, or local term of probation, supervised release, or parole for another offense to which the defendant is subject or becomes subject during the term of probation. A term of probation does not run while the defendant is imprisoned in connection with a conviction for a Federal, State, or local crime unless the imprisonment is for a period of less than thirty consecutive days.

(c) Early Termination.— The court, after considering the factors set forth in section 3553 (a) to the extent that they are applicable, may, pursuant to the provisions of the Federal Rules of Criminal Procedure relating to the modification of probation, terminate a term of probation previously ordered and discharge the defendant at any time in the case of a misdemeanor or an infraction or at any time after the expiration of one year of probation in the case of a felony, if it is satisfied that such action is warranted by the conduct of the defendant and the interest of justice.

(d) Extension.— The court may, after a hearing, extend a term of probation, if less than the maximum authorized term was previously imposed, at any time prior to the expiration or termination of the term of probation, pursuant to the provisions applicable to the initial setting of the term of probation.

(e) Subject to Revocation.— A sentence of probation remains conditional and subject to revocation until its expiration or termination.

Source: http://law.onecle.com/uscode/18/3564.html

US Court Rules: http://www.uscourts.gov/RulesAndPolicies.aspx

US Courts: http://www.uscourts.gov

Florida:

*Note: You must follow the Florida Rules to have your probation terminated early. The following site offers a form and instructions to terminate probation early in Florida: http://pd13.state.fl.us/PDF/pro-se-terminate-probation.pdf

Florida Criminal Procedure and Corrections, Chapter 948, Probation and Community Control Sections 948.04 to 948.05.

Florida Statutes 948.04: Period of probation; duty of probationer; early termination.--

(1) Defendants found guilty of felonies who are placed on probation shall be under supervision not to exceed 2 years unless otherwise specified by the court. No defendant placed on probation pursuant to s. 948.012(1) or s. 948.034 is subject to the probation limitations of this subsection. A defendant who is placed on probation or community control for a violation of chapter 794 or chapter 827 is subject to the maximum level of supervision provided by the supervising agency, and that supervision shall continue through the full term of the court-imposed probation or community control.

(2) Upon the termination of the period of probation, the probationer shall be released from probation and is not liable to sentence for the offense for which probation was allowed. During the period of probation, the probationer shall perform the terms and conditions of his or her probation.

(3) If the probationer has performed satisfactorily, has not been found in violation of any terms or conditions of supervision, and has met all financial sanctions imposed by the court, including, but not limited to, fines, court costs, and

restitution, the Department of Corrections may recommend early termination of probation to the court at any time before the scheduled termination date.

948.05 Court to admonish or commend probationer or offender in community control.--A court may at any time cause a probationer or offender in community control to appear before it to be admonished or commended, and, when satisfied that its action will be for the best interests of justice and the welfare of society, it may discharge the probationer or offender in community control from further supervision.

Source: http://law.justia.com/florida/codes/TitleXLVII/ch0948.html

*Must follow the Florida rules to ask for early termination of probation in Florida.

*The following site offers a form and instructions to terminate probation early in Florida: http://pd13.state.fl.us/PDF/pro-se-terminate-probation.pdf

Florida State Courts: http://www.flcourts.org/

Georgia:

Georgia Code – Criminal Procedure – Title 17, Section 17-10-1

(5)(A) Where a defendant has been sentenced to probation, the court shall retain jurisdiction throughout the period of the probated sentence as provided for in subsection (g) of Code Section 42-8-34. Without limiting the generality of the foregoing, the court may shorten the period of probation on motion of the defendant or on its own motion, if the court determines that probation is no longer necessary or appropriate for the ends of justice, the protection of society, and the rehabilitation of the defendant. Prior to entering any order for shortening a period of probation, the court shall afford notice to the victim or victims of all sex related offenses or violent offenses resulting in serious bodily injury or death, and, upon request of the victim or victims so notified, shall afford notice and an opportunity for hearing to the defendant and the prosecuting attorney.

Last modified: April 25, 2006

Source: http://law.onecle.com/georgia/17/17-10-1.html

Link to Probation Services Handbook in Georgia:

http://www.statecourt.org/criminal_forms/probation_hndbk.pdf

Georgia Judicial Branch: http://www.georgiacourts.gov/

Hawaii:

Hawaii Revised Statutes, Section 706-630

Hawaii Revised Statutes §706-630 Discharge of defendant. Upon the termination of the period of the probation or the earlier discharge of the defendant, the defendant shall be relieved of any obligations imposed by the order of the court and shall have satisfied the disposition of the court, except as to any action under this chapter to collect unpaid fines, restitution, attorney's fees, costs, or interest. [L 1972, c 9, pt of §1; am L 1986, c 314, §31; am L 1998, c 269, §5]

 Source: http://www.capitol.hawaii.gov/hrscurrent/Vol14_Ch0701-0853/HRS0706/HRS_0706-0630.htm

Hawaii State Judiciary: http://www.courts.state.hi.us/

Idaho:

Idaho Code, Title 19 – Criminal Procedure, Chapter 26 – Suspension of Judgment and Sentence and Parole Offenders

TITLE 19

CRIMINAL PROCEDURE

CHAPTER 26

SUSPENSION OF JUDGMENT AND SENTENCE

AND PAROLE OFFENDERS

Idaho Code Section 19-2604. DISCHARGE OF DEFENDANT -- AMENDMENT OF JUDGMENT. (1) If sentence has been imposed but suspended, or if sentence has been withheld, upon application of the defendant and upon satisfactory showing that the defendant has at all times complied with the terms and conditions upon which he was placed on probation, or has successfully completed and graduated from an authorized drug court program or mental health court program and has at all times complied with the terms and conditions of probation during any period of probation that may have been served following such graduation, the court may, if convinced by the showing made that there is no longer cause for continuing the period of probation, and if it be compatible with the public interest, terminate the sentence or set aside the plea of guilty or conviction of the defendant, and finally dismiss the case and discharge the defendant; and this shall apply to the cases in which defendants have been convicted and granted probation by the court before this law goes into effect, as well as to cases which arise thereafter. The final dismissal of the case as herein provided shall have the effect of restoring the defendant to his civil rights.

Source: http://law.justia.com/idaho/codes/19ftoc/190260004.html

Link to Idaho Court Rules: http://www.the3rdjudicialdistrict.com/

Idaho State Judiciary: http://www.isc.idaho.gov/courtfor.htm

Illinois:

Illinois 730, ILCS 5 Unified Code of Corrections, Article 6, Sentences of Probation and Conditional Discharge

(730 ILCS 5/Ch. V Art. 6 heading)

ARTICLE 6. SENTENCES OF PROBATION AND CONDITIONAL DISCHARGE

(730 ILCS 5/5-6-1) (from Ch. 38, par. 1005-6-1)

(Text of Section from P.A. 94-169)

Sec. 5-6-1. Sentences of Probation and of Conditional Discharge and Disposition of Supervision. The General Assembly finds that in order to protect the public, the criminal justice system must compel compliance with the conditions of probation by responding to violations with swift, certain and fair punishments and intermediate sanctions. The Chief Judge of each circuit shall adopt a system of structured, intermediate sanctions for violations of the terms and conditions of a sentence of probation, conditional discharge or disposition of supervision.

(a) Except where specifically prohibited by other provisions of this Code, the court shall impose a sentence of probation or conditional discharge upon an offender unless, having regard to the nature and circumstance of the offense, and to the history, character and condition of the offender, the court is of the opinion that:

(1) his imprisonment or periodic imprisonment is necessary for the protection of the public; or (2) probation or conditional discharge would deprecate the seriousness of the offender's conduct and would be inconsistent with the ends of justice; or (3) a combination of imprisonment with concurrent or consecutive probation when an offender has been admitted into a drug court program under Section 20 of the Drug Court Treatment Act is necessary for the protection of the public and for the rehabilitation of the offender.

The court shall impose as a condition of a sentence of probation, conditional discharge, or supervision, that the probation agency may invoke any sanction from the list of intermediate sanctions adopted by the chief judge of the circuit court for violations of the terms and conditions of the sentence of probation, conditional discharge, or supervision, subject to the provisions of Section 5-6-4 of this Act.

(b) The court may impose a sentence of conditional discharge for an offense if the court is of the opinion that neither a sentence of imprisonment nor of periodic imprisonment nor of probation supervision is appropriate.

(c) The court may, upon a plea of guilty or a stipulation by the defendant of the facts supporting the charge or a finding of guilt, defer further proceedings and the imposition of a sentence, and enter an order for supervision of the defendant, if the defendant is not charged with: (i) a Class A misdemeanor, as defined by the following provisions of the Criminal Code of 1961: Sections 11-9.1; 12-3.2; 12-15; 26-5; 31-1; 31-6; 31-7; subsections (b) and (c) of Section 21-1; paragraph (1) through (5), (8), (10), and (11) of subsection (a) of Section 24-1; (ii) a Class A misdemeanor violation of Section 3.01, 3.03-1, or 4.01 of the Humane Care for Animals Act; or (iii) felony. If the defendant is not barred from receiving an order for supervision as provided in this subsection, the court may enter an order for supervision after considering the circumstances of the offense, and the history, character and condition of the offender, if the court is of the opinion that:

(1) the offender is not likely to commit further crimes; (2) the defendant and the public would be best served if the defendant were not to receive a criminal record; and (3) in the best interests of justice an order of
supervision is more appropriate than a sentence otherwise permitted under this Code.

Source: http://law.justia.com/illinois/codes/chapter55/61715.html

Official site of the Illinois Courts http://www.state.il.us/court/

Indiana:

Indiana Code 35-38-2 Chapter 2 - Probation

Indiana Code Section 35-38-2-1
Conditions of probation; advice on violation specification in record; administrative costs; transfer of three percent of probation user's fee; administrative fee; user's fee; collection of administrative fee; disposition of money collected; supplemental adult probation services fund; payment by credit card; credit card service fee

Sec. 1. (a) Whenever it places a person on probation, the court shall:

(1) specify in the record the conditions of the probation; and

(2) advise the person that if the person violates a condition of probation during the probationary period, a petition to revoke probation may be filed before the earlier of the following:

(A) One (1) year after the termination of probation.

(B) Forty-five (45) days after the state receives notice of the violation.

(b) In addition, if the person was convicted of a felony and is placed on probation, the court shall order the person to pay to the probation department the user's fee prescribed under subsection (d). If the person was convicted of a misdemeanor, the court may order the person to pay the user's fee prescribed under subsection (e). The court may:

(1) modify the conditions (except a fee payment may only be modified as provided in section 1.7(b) of this chapter); or

(2) terminate the probation; at any time. If the person commits an additional crime, the court may revoke the probation.

Source: http://www.in.gov/legislative/ic/code/title35/ar38/ch2.html

Indiana Courts: http://www.in.gov/judiciary/

Iowa:

Iowa Criminal Code Section 907.9 Discharge from Probation:

1. At any time that the court determines that the purposes of probation have been fulfilled and the fees imposed under section 905.14 have been paid or on condition that unpaid supervision fees be paid, the court may order the discharge of a person from probation.

2. At any time that a probation officer determines that the purposes of probation have been fulfilled and the fees imposed under section 905.14 have been paid or on condition that unpaid supervision fees be paid, the officer may order the discharge of a person from probation after approval of the district director and

notification of the sentencing court and the county attorney who prosecuted the case.

3. The sentencing judge may order a hearing on its own motion, or shall order a hearing upon the request of the county attorney, for review of such discharge. If the sentencing judge is no longer serving or unable to order such hearing, the chief judge of the district or the chief judge's designee shall order any hearing pursuant to this section. Following the hearing, the court shall approve or rescind such discharge. If a hearing is not ordered within thirty days after notification by the probation officer, the person shall be discharged and the probation officer shall notify the state court administrator of such discharge.

Source: http://www.legis.state.ia.us/IACODE/2003SUPPLEMENT/907/9.html

Iowa Judicial Branch: http://www.iowacourts.gov/

Kansas:

Kansas Statutes: Chapter 21, Article 46 Section 11

Section 21-4611: Period of suspension of sentence, probation or assignment to community corrections; parole of misdemeanant; duration of probation in felony cases, modification or extension. (a) The period of suspension of sentence, probation or assignment to community corrections fixed by the court shall not exceed five years in felony cases involving crimes committed prior to July 1, 1993, or two years in misdemeanor cases, subject to renewal and extension for additional fixed periods not exceeding five years in such felony cases, nor two years in misdemeanor cases. In no event shall the total period of probation, suspension of sentence or assignment to community corrections for a felony committed prior to July 1, 1993, exceed the greatest maximum term provided by law for the crime, except that where the defendant is convicted of nonsupport of a child, the period may be continued as long as the responsibility for support continues. Probation, suspension of sentence or assignment to community corrections may be terminated by the court at any time and upon such termination or upon termination by expiration of the term of probation, suspension of sentence or assignment to community corrections, an order to this effect shall be entered by the court. The provisions of K.S.A. 75-5291, and amendments thereto, shall be applicable to any assignment to a community correctional services program pursuant to this section.

Source: http://kansasstatutes.lesterama.org/Chapter_21/Article_46/#21-4611

Kansas Judiciary: http://www.kscourts.org/

Kentucky:

Kentucky Revised Statutes 533.020 Probation and conditional discharge.
(1)When a person who has been convicted of an offense or who has entered a plea of guilty to an offense is not sentenced to imprisonment, the court shall place him on probation if he is in need of the supervision, guidance, assistance, or direction that the probation service can provide. Conditions of probation shall be imposed as provided in KRS 533.030, but the court may modify or enlarge the conditions or, if the defendant commits an additional offense or violates a condition, revoke the sentence at any time prior to the expiration or termination of the period of probation. When setting conditions under this subsection, the court shall not order any defendant to pay incarceration costs or any other cost permitted to be ordered under KRS 533.010 or other statute, except restitution and any costs owed to the Department of Corrections, through the circuit clerk.

(2) When a person who has been convicted of an offense or who has entered a plea of guilty to an offense is not sentenced to imprisonment, the court may sentence him to probation with an alternative sentence if it is of the opinion that the defendant should conduct himself according to conditions determined by the court and that probationary supervision alone is insufficient. The court may modify or enlarge the conditions or, if the defendant commits an additional

offense or violates a condition, revoke the sentence at any time prior to the expiration or termination of the alternative sentence.

(3) When a person who has been convicted of an offense or who has entered a plea of guilty to an offense is not sentenced to imprisonment, the court may sentence him to conditional discharge if it is of the opinion that the defendant should conduct himself according to conditions determined by the court but that probationary supervision is inappropriate. Conditions of conditional discharge shall be imposed as provided in KRS 533.030, but the court may modify or enlarge the conditions or, if the defendant commits an additional offense or violates a condition, revoke the sentence at any time prior to the expiration or termination of the period of conditional discharge.

(4) The period of probation, probation with an alternative sentence, or conditional discharge shall be fixed by the court and at any time may be extended or shortened by duly entered court order. Such period, with extensions thereof, shall not exceed five (5) years, or the time necessary to complete restitution, whichever is longer, upon conviction of a felony nor two (2) years, or the time necessary to complete restitution, whichever is longer, upon conviction of a misdemeanor. Upon completion of the probationary period, probation with an alternative sentence, or the period of conditional discharge, the defendant shall be deemed finally discharged, provided no warrant issued by the court is pending against him, and probation, probation with an alternative sentence, or conditional discharge has not been revoked.

(5) Notwithstanding the fact that a sentence to probation, probation with an alternative sentence, or conditional discharge can subsequently be modified or revoked, a judgment which includes such a sentence shall constitute a final judgment for purposes of appeal.

Source: http://law.justia.com/kentucky/codes/533-00/020.html

Kentucky Courts: http://courts.ky.gov/

Louisiana:

Louisiana Code of Criminal Procedure (CCPR) Article 897:

Termination of probation or suspended sentence; discharge of defendant In a felony case the court may terminate the defendant's probation and discharge him at any time after the expiration of one year of probation.

In a misdemeanor case the court may terminate the defendant's suspended sentence or probation and discharge him at any time.

Source: http://www.legis.state.la.us/lss/lss.asp?doc=112898

Louisiana Code of Criminal Procedure Article (CCPR) Article 898:

Satisfaction of suspended sentence and probation

Upon completion of the period of suspension of sentence or probation, or an earlier discharge of the defendant pursuant to Article 897, the defendant shall have satisfied the sentence imposed. Where part of a sentence is suspended, this provision shall not apply until the unsuspended part has been satisfied.

Source: http://www.legis.state.la.us/lss/lss.asp?doc=112899

Louisiana Courts: http://www.louisiana.gov/Government/Judicial_Branch/

Maine:

Title 17-A: MAINE CRIMINAL CODE Part 3:
Chapter 49: PROBATION HEADING: PL 2003, C. 688, PT. A, §13 (RPR)

Title 17 §1202. Period of probation; modification and discharge

2.   During the period of probation specified in the sentence made pursuant to subsection 1, and upon application of a person on probation or the person's probation officer, or upon its own motion, the court may, after a hearing upon

notice to the probation officer and the person on probation, modify the requirements imposed by the court or a community reparations board, add further requirements authorized by section 1204 or relieve the person on probation of any requirement imposed by the court or a community reparations board that, in its opinion, imposes on the person an unreasonable burden. If the person on probation cannot meet a requirement imposed by the court or a community reparations board, the person shall bring a motion under this subsection. Notwithstanding this subsection, the court may grant, ex parte, a motion brought by the probation officer to add further requirements if the requirements are immediately necessary to protect the safety of an individual or the public and if all reasonable efforts have been made to give written or oral notice to the person on probation. Any requirements added pursuant to an ex parte motion do not take effect until written notice of the requirements, along with written notice of the scheduled date, time and place when the court shall hold a hearing on the added requirements, is given to the person on probation.

[2005, c. 265, §8 (AMD) .]

2-A.   Once the period of probation has commenced, on motion of the probation officer, or of the person on probation, or on the court's own motion, the court may convert at any time a period of probation for a Class D or Class E crime or a Class C crime under Title 29-A, section 2557 to a period of administrative release. A conversion to administrative release may not be ordered unless notice of the motion is given to the probation officer and the attorney for the State. The provisions of chapter 54-G apply when probation is converted to administrative release. Conversion to administrative release serves to relieve the person on probation of any obligations imposed by the probation conditions.

[2005, c. 265, §9 (AMD) .]

3.   Once the period of probation has commenced, on motion of the probation officer, or of the person on probation, or on its own motion, the court may terminate at any time a period of probation and discharge the convicted person at any time earlier than that provided in the sentence made pursuant to subsection 1, if warranted by the conduct of such person. A termination and discharge may

not be ordered unless notice of the motion is given to the probation officer and the attorney for the State. Such termination and discharge serves to relieve the person on probation of any obligations imposed by the sentence of probation.
[2005, c. 265, §10 (AMD) .]

3-A. A motion and hearing pursuant to subsection 2, 2-A or 3 need not be before the justice or judge who originally imposed probation. Any justice or judge may initiate and hear a motion and any justice or judge may hear a motion brought by the probation officer or by the person on probation.
[2009, c. 336, §14 (NEW) .]

4.   Any justice, in order to comply with section 1256, subsection 8, may terminate a period of probation that would delay commencement of a consecutive unsuspended term of imprisonment. Any judge may also do so if that judge has jurisdiction over each of the sentences involved.
[1989, c. 739, §1 (NEW) .]

Source: http://www.mainelegislature.org/legis/Statutes/17-A/title17-Asec1202.html

Maine Judiciary: http://www.courts.state.me.us/

Maryland:

Maryland Criminal Procedure Section 6-225:

(b)   (1)   (i)   Probation may be granted whether the crime is punishable by fine or imprisonment or both.

(ii)   If the crime is punishable by both fine and imprisonment, the court may impose a fine and place the defendant on probation as to the imprisonment.

(iii)   Probation may be limited to one or more counts or indictments but, in the absence of express limitation, extends to the entire sentence and judgment.

(iv)   The court may revoke or modify a condition of probation or may reduce the period of probation.

(v)   As a condition of probation, the court may order a defendant to a term of custodial confinement.

(2)   If a sentence of imprisonment is imposed and a part of it is suspended with the defendant placed on probation, the court may impose as a condition of probation that the probation begin on the day the defendant is released from imprisonment.

(c)   If the court places on probation a defendant who has been convicted of a violation of any provision of Title 5 of the Criminal Law Article, the court shall require as a condition that the defendant participate in a drug treatment or education program approved by the Department of Health and Mental Hygiene, unless the court finds and states on the record that the interests of the defendant and the public do not require the imposition of this condition.

(d)   The court may impose a sentence of custodial confinement or imprisonment as a condition of probation.

(e)   If an individual violates the terms of probation, any time served by the individual in custodial confinement shall be credited against any sentence of incarceration imposed by the court.

Source: http://law.justia.com/maryland/codes/gcp/6-225.html

Maryland Judiciary: http://www.courts.state.md.us/

Massachusetts:

General Laws of Massachusetts – Chapter 279 Judgment and Execution. – Section 1 Suspension of execution; payment of fine; probation; revocation of suspension; exceptions

Section 1A. When a person convicted before a court is sentenced to fine and imprisonment, the court may direct that the execution of the sentence, or any part thereof, be suspended, and that he be placed on probation for such time and on such terms and conditions as it shall fix. The court may direct, as one of such terms and conditions, that payment of the fine may be made to the probation officer in one payment, or in part payments, during the period of probation or any extension thereof, and when such fine shall have been fully paid the order of commitment as to the fine shall be void, but the order of commitment as to imprisonment shall not be affected by such payment. The probation officer shall give a receipt for every payment so made, shall keep a record of the same, shall pay the fine, or all sums received in part payment thereof, to the clerk of the court at the end of the period of probation or any extension thereof, and shall keep on file the clerk's receipt therefor. If during or at the end of said period the probation officer shall report that the fine is in whole or in part unpaid, and in his opinion the person is unwilling or unable to pay it, the court may either extend said period, place the case on file or revoke the suspension of the execution of the sentence. When such suspension is revoked, in a case where the fine has been paid in part, the defendant may be committed for default in payment of the balance, and may also be committed for the term of imprisonment fixed in the original sentence. This section shall not permit the suspension of the execution of the sentence of any person convicted of a crime punishable by imprisonment for life or of a crime an element of which is being armed with a dangerous weapon, or of any person convicted of any other felony if it shall appear that he has been previously convicted of any felony. In granting probation under this section, the court shall include in its terms and conditions of probation that the person convicted shall pay any child support due under a support order, as defined in section 1A of chapter 119A, including payment toward any arrearage of support that accrues or has accrued or compliance with any payment plan between the person convicted and the IV-D agency as set forth in said chapter 119A.

Source: http://law.justia.com/massachusetts/codes/gl-pt4-toc/279-1.html

Massachusetts Court System: http://www.mass.gov/courts/

Michigan:

Michigan Mich. Comp. Laws § 771.2

Chapter 771.2 Probation period; order fixing period and conditions of probation; registration pursuant to sex offenders registration act; reduction in probation period; subsection (1) inapplicable to certain juveniles.

Sec. 2.

(1) Except as provided in section 2a of this chapter, if the defendant is convicted for an offense that is not a felony, the probation period shall not exceed 2 years. Except as provided in section 2a of this chapter, if the defendant is convicted of a felony, the probation period shall not exceed 5 years.

(2) The court shall by order, to be filed or entered in the cause as the court may direct by general rule or in each case, fix and determine the period and conditions of probation. The order is part of the record in the cause. The court may amend the order in form or substance at any time.

(3) A defendant who was placed on probation under section 1(4) of this chapter prior to the effective date of the act that amended this section is subject to the conditions of probation specified in section 3 of this chapter, including payment of a probation supervision fee as prescribed in section 3c of this chapter, and to revocation for violation of these conditions, but the probation period shall not be

reduced other than by a revocation that results in imprisonment or as otherwise provided by law.

(4) If an individual is placed on probation for a listed offense enumerated in section 2 of the sex offenders registration act, 1994 PA 295, MCL 28.722, the individual's probation officer shall register the individual or accept the individual's registration as provided in that act.

(5) Subsection (1) does not apply to a juvenile placed on probation and committed under section 1(3) or (4) of chapter IX to an institution or agency described in the youth rehabilitation services act, 1974 PA 150, MCL 803.301 to 803.309.

Source: http://law.justia.com/michigan/codes/mcl-chapters-760-777/mcl-771-2.html

Michigan Courts: http://courts.michigan.gov/

*Form: MC 245 (5/07) **MOTION AND ORDER FOR DISCHARGE FROM PROBATION** http://courts.michigan.gov/scao/courtforms/probation/mc245.pdf

Minnesota:

2009 Minnesota Statues 609.3751 Discharge and Dismissal

Subdivision 1. Applicability.

A person is eligible for a discharge and dismissal under this section, if the person:

(1) has not been previously convicted of a felony under the laws of this state or elsewhere;

(2) has not been previously convicted of a violation of section 609.375 or of a similar offense in this state or elsewhere;

(3) has not previously participated in or completed a diversion program relating to a charge of violating section609.375; and

(4) has not previously been placed on probation without a judgment of guilty for violation of section 609.375.

Subd. 2. *Procedure*

For a person eligible under subdivision 1 who is charged with violating section 609.375, the court may after trial or upon a plea of guilty, without entering a judgment of guilty and with the consent of the person, defer further proceedings and place the person on probation upon such reasonable conditions as it may require and for a period not to exceed the maximum sentence provided for the violation. At a minimum, the conditions must require the defendant to:

(1) provide the public authority responsible for child support enforcement with an affidavit attesting to the defendant's present address, occupation, employer, current income, assets, and account information, as defined in section 13B.06; and

(2) execute a written payment agreement regarding both current support and arrearages that is approved by the court.

In determining whether to approve a payment agreement under clause (2), the court shall apply the provisions of chapter 518A consistent with the obligor's ability to pay.

Subd. 3. **Violation**.

Upon violation of a condition of the probation, including a failure to comply with the written payment agreement approved by the court under subdivision 2, clause (2), the court may enter an adjudication of guilt and proceed as otherwise provided in law.

Subd. 4. **Early Dismissal.**

The court may, in its discretion, dismiss the proceedings against the person and discharge the person from probation before the expiration of the maximum period prescribed for the person's probation but may do so only if the full amount of any arrearages has been brought current.

Source: https://www.revisor.mn.gov/statutes/?id=609.3751

Minnesota Judicial Branch: http://www.mncourts.gov/

Mississippi:

Mississippi Code SEC. 47-7-35. Terms and conditions of probation; court to determine.

The courts referred to in Section 47-7-33 or 47-7-34 shall determine the terms and conditions of probation or post-release supervision and may alter or modify, at any time during the period of probation or post-release supervision the conditions and may include among them the following or any other:

That the, offender shall:

(a) Commit no offense against the laws of this or any other state of the United States, or of the United States;

(b) Avoid injurious or vicious habits;

(c) Avoid persons or places of disreputable or harmful character;

(d) Report to the probation and parole officer as directed;

(e) Permit the probation and parole officer to visit him at home or elsewhere;

(f) Work faithfully at suitable employment so far as possible;

(g) Remain within a specified area;

(h) Pay his fine in one (1) or several sums;

(i) Support his dependents;

(j) Submit, as provided in Section 47-5-601, to any type of breath, saliva or urine chemical analysis test, the purpose of which is to detect the possible presence of alcohol or a substance prohibited or controlled by any law of the State of Mississippi or the United States.

Source: http://www.mscode.com/free/statutes/47/007/0035.htm

Mississippi Judiciary: http://www.mssc.state.ms.us/

Mississippi Code SEC. 47-7-37. Period of probation; arrest, revocation and recommitment for violation of probation or post-release supervision.

The period of probation shall be fixed by the court, and may at any time be extended or terminated by the court, or judge in vacation. Such period with any extension thereof shall not exceed five (5) years, except that in cases of desertion and/or failure to support minor children, the period of probation may be fixed and/or extended by the court for so long as the duty to support such minor children exists.

At any time during the period of probation the court, or judge in vacation, may issue a warrant for violating any of the conditions of probation or suspension of sentence and cause the probationer to be arrested. Any probation and parole officer may arrest a probationer without a warrant, or may deputize any other officer with power of arrest to do so by giving him a written statement setting forth that the probationer has, in the judgment of the probation and parole officer, violated the conditions of probation. Such written statement delivered with the probationer by the arresting officer to the official in charge of a county jail or other place of detention shall be sufficient warrant for the detention of the probationer.

Source: http://www.mscode.com/free/statutes/47/007/0037.htm

Mississippi Judiciary: http://www.mssc.state.ms.us/

Missouri:

Chapter 559 — Probation> § 559.036. — Duration of probation--revocation.

559.036. 1. A term of probation commences on the day it is imposed. Multiple terms of Missouri probation, whether imposed at the same time or at different times, shall run concurrently. Terms of probation shall also run concurrently with any federal or other state jail, prison, probation or parole term for another offense to which the defendant is or becomes subject during the period, unless otherwise specified by the Missouri court.

2. The court may terminate a period of probation and discharge the defendant at any time before completion of the specific term fixed under section 559.016 if warranted by the conduct of the defendant and the ends of justice. The court may extend the term of the probation, but no more than one extension of any probation may be ordered except that the court may extend the term of probation by one additional year by order of the court if the defendant admits he or she has violated the conditions of probation or is found by the court to have violated the conditions of his or her probation. Total time on any probation term, including any extension shall not exceed the maximum term established in section 559.016. Procedures for termination, discharge and extension may be established by rule of court.

Source: http://law.justia.com/missouri/codes/t38/5590000036.html

Missouri Judiciary: http://www.courts.mo.gov/

Montana:

Mont Code Ann Section 46-23-1011: Montana Code – Supervision On Probation

(1) The department shall supervise probationers during their probation period, including supervision after release from imprisonment imposed pursuant to

45-5-503(4), 45-5-507(5), 45-5-601(3), 45-5-602(3), 45-5-603(2)(c), or 45-5-625(4), in accord with the conditions set by a sentencing judge. If the sentencing judge did not set conditions of probation at the time of sentencing, the court shall, at the request of the department, hold a hearing and set conditions of probation. The probationer must be present at the hearing. The probationer has the right to counsel as provided in chapter 8 of this title.

(2) A copy of the conditions of probation must be signed by the probationer. The department may require a probationer to waive extradition for the probationer's return to Montana.

(3) The probation and parole officer shall regularly advise and consult with the probationer to encourage the probationer to improve the probationer's condition and conduct and shall inform the probationer of the restoration of rights on successful completion of the sentence.

(4) (a) The probation and parole officer may recommend and a judge may modify or add any condition of probation or suspension of sentence at any time.

(b) The probation and parole officer shall provide the county attorney in the sentencing jurisdiction with a report that identifies the conditions of probation and the reason why the officer believes that the judge should modify or add the conditions.

(c) The county attorney may file a petition requesting that the court modify or add conditions as requested by the probation and parole officer.

(d) The court may grant the petition if the probationer does not object. If the probationer objects to the petition, the court shall hold a hearing pursuant to the provisions of 46-18-203.

(e) Except as they apply to supervision after release from imprisonment imposed pursuant to 45-5-503(4), 45-5-507(5), 45-5-601(3), 45-5-602(3), 45-5-603(2)(c), or 45-5-625(4), the provisions of 46-18-203(7)(a)(ii) do not apply to this section.

(f) The probationer shall sign a copy of new or modified conditions of probation. The court may waive or modify a condition of restitution only as provided in 46-18-246.

(5) (a) Upon recommendation of the probation and parole officer, a judge may conditionally discharge a probationer from supervision before expiration of the probationer's sentence if:

(i) the judge determines that a conditional discharge from supervision:

(A) is in the best interests of the probationer and society; and

(B) will not present unreasonable risk of danger to the victim of the offense; and

(ii) the offender has paid all restitution and court-ordered financial obligations in full.

(b) Subsection (5)(a) does not prohibit a judge from revoking the order suspending execution or deferring imposition of sentence, as provided in 46-18-203, for a probationer who has been conditionally discharged from supervision.

(c) If the department certifies to the sentencing judge that the workload of a district probation and parole office has exceeded the optimum workload for the district over the preceding 60 days, the judge may not place an offender on probation under supervision by that district office unless the judge grants a conditional discharge to a probationer being supervised by that district office. The department may recommend probationers to the judge for conditional discharge. The judge may accept or reject the recommendations of the department. The department shall determine the optimum workload for each district probation and parole office.

Source: http://codes.lp.findlaw.com/mtcode/46/23/10/46-23-1011

Montana Judiciary: http://courts.mt.gov/default.mcpx

Nebraska:

Law> Nebraska Law> Nebraska Code> Chapter 29 — Criminal Procedure> § 29-2263 — Probation; term; court; powers; probation obligation satisfied, when; probationer outside of jurisdiction without permission; effect.

Nebraska Code Section 29-2263

Probation; term; court; powers; probation obligation satisfied, when; probationer outside of jurisdiction without permission; effect.

(1) When a court has sentenced an offender to probation, the court shall specify the term of such probation which shall be not more than five years upon conviction of a felony or second offense misdemeanor and two years upon conviction of a first offense misdemeanor. The court, on application of a probation officer or of the offender or on its own motion, may discharge an offender at any time.

(2) During the term of probation, the court on application of a probation officer or of the offender, or its own motion, may modify or eliminate any of the conditions imposed on the offender or add further conditions authorized by section 29-2262. This subsection does not preclude a probation officer from imposing administrative sanctions with the offender's full knowledge and consent as authorized by subsection (2) of section 29-2266.

(3) Upon completion of the term of probation, or the earlier discharge of the offender, the offender shall be relieved of any obligations imposed by the order of the court and shall have satisfied the sentence for his or her crime.

(4) Whenever a probationer disappears or leaves the jurisdiction of the court without permission, the time during which he or she keeps his or her whereabouts hidden or remains away from the jurisdiction of the court shall be added to the original term of probation.

Annotations:

Terms of probation may be terminated, modified, or extended under lawful limits by the trial court. State v. Sock, 227 Neb. 646, 419 N.W.2d 525 (1988).

Source: http://law.justia.com/nebraska/codes/s29index/s2922063000.html

Nebraska Judicial Branch: http://www.supremecourt.ne.gov/

Nevada:

DISCHARGE

Nebraska Revised Statutes, Chapter 176A Section 850

NRS 176A.850 Honorable discharge from probation: When granted; restoration of civil rights; effect; documentation.

1. A person who:

(a) Has fulfilled the conditions of his probation for the entire period thereof;

(b) Is recommended for earlier discharge by the Division; or

(c) Has demonstrated his fitness for honorable discharge but because of economic hardship, verified by the Division, has been unable to make restitution as ordered by the court, may be granted an honorable discharge from probation by order of the court.

2. Any amount of restitution remaining unpaid constitutes a civil liability arising upon the date of discharge.

3. Except as otherwise provided in subsection 4, a person who has been honorably discharged from probation:

(a) Is free from the terms and conditions of his probation.

(b) Is immediately restored to the following civil rights:

(1) The right to vote; and

(2) The right to serve as a juror in a civil action.

Source:http://law.justia.com/nevada/codes/NRS-176A.html#NRS176ASec850

Nevada Judiciary: http://www.nevadajudiciary.us

New Hampshire:

Law> New Hampshire Law> New Hampshire Code> TITLE LI — COURTS (Includes Chapters 490 - 505)> CHAPTER 504-A: PROBATIONERS AND PAROLEES> Section 504-A:3 Termination of Probation or Parole.

New Hampshire Code, Section 504-A:3 Termination of Probation or Parole.

The authority that placed a person on probation or parole may terminate the probation or parole at any time.

Source: http://law.justia.com/newhampshire/codes/nhtoc-li/504-a-3.html

New Hampshire Judicial Branch: http://www.courts.state.nh.us/

New Jersey:

New Jersey Permanent Statutes Database

Title 2C The New Jersey Code of Criminal Justice

   2C:45-2. Period of Suspension or Probation; Modification of Conditions; Discharge of Defendant

   a.   When the court has suspended imposition of sentence or has sentenced a defendant to be placed on probation, the period of the suspension shall be fixed by the court at not to exceed the maximum term which could have been imposed or more than 5 years whichever is lesser. The period of probation shall be fixed by the court at not less than 1 year nor more than 5 years. The court, on application of a probation officer or of the defendant, or on its own motion, may discharge the defendant at any time.

b.   During the period of the suspension or probation, the court, on application of a probation officer or of the defendant, or on its own motion, may (1) modify the requirements imposed on the defendants; or (2) add further requirements authorized by N.J.S.2C:45-1. The court shall eliminate any requirement that imposes an unreasonable burden on the defendant.

c.   Upon the termination of the period of suspension or probation or the earlier discharge of the defendant, the defendant shall be relieved of any obligations imposed by the order of the court and shall have satisfied his sentence for the offense unless the defendant has failed:

Source: http://lis.njleg.state.nj.us

New Jersey Judiciary: http://www.judiciary.state.nj.us/

New Mexico:

Law> New Mexico Law> New Mexico Code> Chapter 31 — Criminal Procedure.> Article 21 — Sentence, Pardons and Paroles, 31-21-1 through 31-21-27.> Section 31-21-21 — Conditions of probation.

New Mexico Statutes 31-21-21. Conditions of probation.

The board shall adopt general regulations concerning the conditions of probation which apply in the absence of specific conditions imposed by the court. All probationers are subject to supervision of the board unless otherwise specifically ordered by the court in the particular case. Nothing in the Probation and Parole Act [31-21-3 to 31-21-19 NMSA 1978] limits the authority of the court to impose or modify any general or specific condition of probation. The board may recommend and by order the court may impose and modify any conditions of probation. The court shall transmit to the board and to the probationer a copy of any order.

Source: http://law.justia.com/newmexico/codes/nmrc/jd_31-21-21-d1fb.html

New Mexico Judiciary: http://www.nmcourts.gov/

New York:

Law> New York Law> New York Code> Criminal Procedure> Sentences Of Probation, Conditional Discharge And Parole Supervision> Termination Of Sentence.

New York Criminal Procedure § 410.90 Termination of sentence.

1. The court may at any time terminate either a period of probation, other than a period of lifetime probation, for conviction to a crime or a period of conditional discharge for an offense.

2. The court may terminate a period of probation for a person who is subject to lifetime probation and who has been on unrevoked probation for at least five consecutive years.

3. (a) The court shall grant a request for termination of a sentence of probation under this section when, having regard to the conduct and condition of the probationer, the court is of the opinion that:

(i) the probationer is no longer in need of such guidance, training or other assistance which would otherwise be administered through probation supervision;

(ii) the probationer has diligently complied with the terms and conditions of the sentence of probation; and

(iii) the termination of the sentence of probation is not adverse to the protection of the public.

No such termination shall be granted unless the court is satisfied that the probationer, who is otherwise financially able to comply with an order of restitution or reparation, has made a good faith effort to comply therewith.

(b) The court shall grant a request for termination of a sentence of conditional discharge under this section when, having regard to the conduct and condition of the defendant, the court is of the opinion that:

(i) the defendant has diligently complied with the terms and conditions of the sentence of conditional discharge; and

(ii) termination of the sentence of conditional discharge is not adverse to protection of the public.

Source: http://law.justia.com/newyork/codes/criminal-procedure/cpl0410.90_410.90.html

New York State Unified Court System: http://www.courts.state.ny.us/

North Carolina:

Law> North Carolina Law> North Carolina Code> Chapter 15A — Criminal Procedure Act.> North Carolina General Statutes 15A-1342. Incidents of probation.

North Carolina General Statutes 15A-1342. Incidents of probation.

(a) Period. The court may place a convicted offender on probation for the appropriate period as specified in G.S. 15A-1343.2(d), not to exceed a maximum of five years. The court may place a defendant as to whom prosecution has been deferred on probation for a maximum of two years. The probation remains conditional and subject to revocation during the period of probation imposed, unless terminated as provided in subsection (b) or G.S. 15A-1341(c).

Extension. The court with the consent of the defendant may extend the period of probation beyond the original period (i) for the purpose of allowing the defendant to complete a program of restitution, or (ii) to allow the defendant to continue medical or psychiatric treatment ordered as a condition of the probation. The period of extension shall not exceed three years beyond the original period of probation. The special extension authorized herein may be ordered only in the last six months of the original period of probation. Any probationary judgment form provided to a defendant on supervised probation shall state that probation may be extended pursuant to this subsection.

(b) Early Termination. The court may terminate a period of probation and discharge the defendant at any time earlier than that provided in subsection (a) if warranted by the conduct of the defendant and the ends of justice.

Source: http://law.justia.com/northcarolina/codes/chapter_15a/gs_15a-1342.html

North Carolina Court System: http://www.nccourts.org/

Form: North Carolina Form AOC-CR-320, Order on Violation of Probation or on Motion to Modify available at:

http://www.nccourts.org/Forms/FormSearchResults.asp

North Dakota:

12.1-32-07.1. Release, discharge, or termination of probation

North Dakota Statutes 12.1-32-06.1. Length and termination of probation – Additional probation for violation of conditions – Penalty.

1.   Except as provided in this section, the length of the period of probation imposed in conjunction with a sentence to probation or a suspended execution or deferred imposition of sentence may not extend for more than five years for a felony and two years for a misdemeanor or infraction from the later of the date of:

     a. The order imposing probation;

b. The defendant's release from incarceration; or

c. Termination of the defendant's parole.

6.   The court may terminate a period of probation and discharge the defendant at any time earlier than provided in subsection 1 if warranted by the of the defendant and the ends of justice.

Source: http://www.legis.nd.gov/information/statutes/cent-code.html

North Dakota Courts: http://www.ndcourts.gov/

Ohio:

Chapter 2951: Probation

Ohio Code 2951.06 Release from Custody upon entry of order of probation.

Upon entry in the records of the judge or magistrate of the sentence of a community control sanction provided for in section 2929.15 or 2929.25 of the Revised Code, the defendant shall be released from custody as soon as the requirements and conditions required by the judge supervising the community control sanction have been met. The defendant shall continue under the control and supervision of the appropriate probation agency, to the extent required by law, the conditions of the community control sanction, and the rules and regulations governing the probation agency.

Effective Date: 01-01-2004

Ohio Code 2951.07 Probationary Period

A community control sanction continues for the period that the judge or magistrate determines and, subject to the five-year limit specified in section 2929.15or 2929.25 of the Revised Code, may be extended. If the offender under community control absconds or otherwise leaves the jurisdiction of the court without permission from the probation officer, the probation agency, or the court to do so, or if the offender is confined in any institution for the commission of any offense, the period of community control ceases to run until the time that the offender is brought before the court for its further action.

Effective Date: 01-01-2004

Source: http://codes.ohio.gov/orc/2951

Ohio Judicial System: http://www.supremecourt.ohio.gov/

Oklahoma:

OKLAHOMA STATUTES
TITLE 22.
CRIMINAL PROCEDURE

Oklahoma Statutes §22-982av1. Judicial review.

A. Any time within twelve (12) months after a sentence is imposed or within twelve (12) months after probation has been revoked, the court imposing sentence or revocation of probation may modify such sentence or revocation by directing that another penalty be imposed, if the court is satisfied that the best interests of the public will not be jeopardized. This section shall not apply to convicted felons who have been in confinement in any state prison system for any previous felony conviction during the ten-year period preceding the date that the sentence this section applies to was imposed. Further, without the consent of the district attorney, this section shall not apply to sentences imposed pursuant to a plea agreement.

B. For purposes of judicial review, upon court order or written request from the sentencing judge, the Department of Corrections shall provide the court imposing sentence or revocation of probation with a report to include a summary of the offender's assessed needs, any progress made by the offender in addressing his or her assessed needs, and any other information the Department can supply on the inmate. The court shall consider such reports when modifying the sentence or revocation of probation. The court shall allow the Department of

Corrections at least twenty (20) days after receipt of a request or order from the court to prepare the required reports.

C. If the court considers modification of the sentence or revocation of probation, a hearing shall be made in open court after receipt of the reports required in subsection B of this section. The clerk of the court imposing sentence or revocation of probation shall give notice of the judicial review hearing to the Department of Corrections, the inmate, the inmate's legal counsel, and the district attorney of the county in which the inmate was convicted upon receipt of the reports. Such notice shall be mailed at least twenty-one (21) days prior to the hearing date and shall include a copy of the report and any other written information to be considered at the judicial review hearing.

D. If an appeal is taken from the original sentence or from a revocation of probation which results in a modification of the sentence or modification to the revocation of probation of the defendant, such sentence may be further modified in the manner hereinbefore described within twelve (12) months after the receipt by the clerk of the district court of the mandate from the Supreme Court or the Court of Criminal Appeals.

Source: http://law.justia.com/oklahoma/codes/os22.html

Oklahoma Judicial System: http://www.ok.gov

Oregon:

Oregon Code: 2005: Chapter 137 Judgement and Execution, Parole and Probation by the Court:

137.545 Period of probation; discharge from probation; proceedings in case of violation of conditions. (1) Subject to the limitations in ORS 137.010 and to rules of the Oregon Criminal Justice Commission for felonies committed on or after November 1, 1989:

(a) The period of probation shall be as the court determines and may, in the discretion of the court, be continued or extended.

(b) The court may at any time discharge a person from probation.

Source: http://law.justia.com/oregon/codes/2005/vol4/137.html

Oregon Judicial Department: https://portal.courts.oregon.gov/egov/portal

Pennsylvania:

Modification or revocation of order of probation – 42 Pa. Cons. Stat. Sec. 9771

SUBCHAPTER F

FURTHER JUDICIAL ACTION

Sec.

9771. Modification or revocation of order of probation.

9772. Failure to pay fine.

9773. Modification or revocation of county intermediate punishment sentence.

9774. Revocation of State intermediate punishment sentence.

§ 9771. Modification or revocation of order of probation.

   (a) General rule.--The court may at any time terminate continued supervision or lessen or increase the conditions upon which an order of probation has been imposed.

   (b) Revocation.--The court may revoke an order of probation upon proof of the violation of specified conditions of the probation. Upon revocation the sentencing alternatives available to the court shall be the same as were available at the time of initial sentencing, due consideration being given to the time spent serving the order of probation.

   (c) Limitation on sentence of total confinement.--The court shall not impose a sentence of total confinement upon revocation unless it finds that:

    (1) the defendant has been convicted of another crime;
or

    (2) the conduct of the defendant indicates that it is
likely that he will commit another crime if he is not
imprisoned; or

    (3) such a sentence is essential to vindicate the
authority of the court.

(d) Hearing required.--There shall be no revocation or
increase of conditions of sentence under this section except
after a hearing at which the court shall consider the record of
the sentencing proceeding together with evidence of the conduct
of the defendant while on probation. Probation may be eliminated
or the term decreased without a hearing.

Source:

http://law.onecle.com/pennsylvania/judiciary-and-judicial-
procedure/00.097.071.000.html

The Unified Judicial System of Pennsylvania: http://www.aopc.org

Rhode Island:

Law> Rhode Island Law> Rhode Island Code> Title 12 — Criminal Procedure>
CHAPTER 12-19 — Sentence and Execution>

§ 12-19-8 — Suspension of sentence and probation by superior or district court.

(a) Except where the suspension of sentence shall otherwise be prohibited by
law, whenever any defendant shall appear for sentence before the superior or
district court, the court may impose a sentence and suspend the execution of the
sentence, in whole or in part, or place the defendant on probation without the

imposition of a suspended sentence. The suspension shall place the defendant on probation for the time and on any terms and conditions that the court may fix.

(b) The period of probation, where no sentence is imposed or where sentence is entirely suspended, may be for any period up to the maximum time of sentence provided by applicable statutes. Where sentence is imposed and suspended in part, the term ordered to be served and the period of probation together shall not exceed the maximum time of sentence provided by applicable statutes.

Source: http://law.justia.com/rhodeisland/codes/title12/12-19-8.html

Judiciary of Rhode Island: http://www.courts.ri.gov/

South Carolina:

Title 24 - Corrections, Jails, Probations, Paroles and Pardons
CHAPTER 23.
CASE CLASSIFICATION SYSTEM AND COMMUNITY CORRECTIONS PLAN
ARTICLE 1.
ARTICLE 2.
SENTENCING AND PROBATION PROCEDURES

South Carolina Code SECTION 24-23-130. Termination of supervision.

Upon the satisfactory fulfillment of the conditions of probation, the court, with the recommendation of the agent in charge of the responsible county probation office, may terminate the probationer or supervised prisoner from supervision.

Source: http://www.scstatehouse.gov/CODE/t24c023.htm

South Carolina Judicial Department: http://www.judicial.state.sc.us/

South Dakota:

South Dakota Statute: Chapter 23A-27 Sentence and Judgment

Chapter 23A-27-20.1 Modification of terms and conditions of probation.

23A-27-20.1.   Modification of terms and conditions of probation. The court, upon notice to the probationer, a hearing and good cause, shown, may modify the terms and conditions of a probation which may include extending the probationary period.

Source:

http://legis.state.sd.us/statutes/DisplayStatute.aspx?Type=Statute&Statute=23A-27-20.1

South Dakota Judiciary: http://www.sdjudicial.com/

Tennessee:

Tenn. Code Ann. 40-35-40(c)

The court shall retain full jurisdiction over the defendant during the term of the sentence and may reduce or modify the sentence or may place the defendant on probation supervision where otherwise eligible. Following the first application, applications to reduce or to alter the manner of the service of the sentence may be made at no less than two (2) month intervals.

Source: http://www.michie.com/tennessee

Tennessee Court System: http://www.tsc.state.tn.us/

Texas:

Texas Code of Criminal Procedure, Article 42.12, Section 20. Reduction or Termination of Community Supervision:

(a) At any time, after the defendant has satisfactorily completed one-third of the original community supervision period or two years of community supervision, whichever is less, the period of community supervision may be reduced or terminated by the judge. Upon the satisfactory fulfillment of the conditions of community supervision, and the expiration of the period of community supervision, the judge, by order duly entered, shall amend or modify the original sentence imposed, if necessary, to conform to the community supervision period and shall discharge the defendant. If the judge discharges the defendant under this section, the judge may set aside the verdict or permit the defendant to withdraw his plea, and shall dismiss the accusation, complaint, information or indictment against the defendant, who shall thereafter be released from all penalties and disabilities resulting from the offense or crime of which he has been convicted or to which he has pleaded guilty, except that:

(b) This section does not apply to a defendant convicted of an offense under Sections 49.04-49.08, Penal Code, a defendant convicted of an offense for which on conviction registration as a sex offender is required under Chapter 62, as added by Chapter 668, Acts of the 75th Legislature, Regular Session, 1997, or a defendant convicted of an offense punishable as a state jail felony.

Source: http://www.legis.state.tx.us

Texas Courts Online: http://www.courts.state.tx.us/

Utah:

Utah Code of Criminal Procedure Section 77-18-1. Suspension of sentence -- Pleas held in abeyance -- Probation -- Supervision -- Presentence investigation -- Standards -- Confidentiality -- Terms and conditions -- Termination, revocation, modification, or extension -- Hearings -- Electronic monitoring.

(10) (a) (i) Probation may be terminated at any time at the discretion of the court or upon completion without violation of 36 months probation in felony or class A misdemeanor cases, or 12 months in cases of class B or C

misdemeanors or infractions.

(ii) (A) If, upon expiration or termination of the probation period under Subsection (10)(a)(i), there remains an unpaid balance upon the account receivable as defined in Section **76-3-201.1**, the court may retain jurisdiction of the case and continue the defendant on bench probation for the limited purpose of enforcing the payment of the account receivable.

(B) In accordance with Section **77-18-6**, the court shall record in the registry of civil judgments any unpaid balance not already recorded and immediately transfer responsibility to collect the account to the Office of State Debt Collection.

(iii) Upon motion of the Office of State Debt Collection, prosecutor, victim, or upon its own motion, the court may require the defendant to show cause why his failure to pay should not be treated as contempt of court.

Source: http://law.justia.com/utah/codes/title77/77_14002.html

Utah State Courts: http://www.utcourts.gov/

Vermont:

Vermont Statutes   TITLE 28 Public Institutions and Corrections CHAPTER 5. PROBATION   Subchapter 2. Conditions of Probation; Modifications; Discharge

Vermont Statutes § 251. Duration of probation.

The court placing a person on probation may terminate the period of probation and discharge the person at any time if such termination is warranted by the conduct of the offender and the ends of justice.

Source: http://www.michie.com/vermont/lpext.dll?f=templates&fn=main-h.htm&cp=vtcode

Vermont Judiciary: http://www.vermontjudiciary.org/default.aspx

Virginia:

Law> Virginia Law> Virginia Code> Title 19.2 — CRIMINAL
PROCEDURE.> Chapter 18 - Sentence; Judgment; Execution of Sentence:

Virginia Code of Criminal Procedure § 19.2-304 - Increasing or decreasing probation period and modification of conditions:

The court may subsequently increase or decrease the probation period and may revoke or modify any condition of probation, but only upon a hearing after reasonable notice to both the defendant and the attorney for the Commonwealth.

Source: http://law.justia.com/virginia/codes/toc1902000/19.2-304.html

Virginia Judicial System: http://www.courts.state.va.us/

Washington, DC:

District of Columbia Code: Title 24 Prisoners and Their Treatment: Chapter 3 Probation:

District of Columbia Code § 24-304. Discharge from or continuance of probation; modification or revocation of order [Formerly § 24-104].

(a) Upon the expiration of the term fixed for such probation, the probation officer shall report that fact to the court, with a statement of the conduct of the probationer while on probation, and the court may thereupon discharge the probationer from further supervision, or may extend the probation, as shall seem advisable. At any time during the probationary term the court may modify the terms and conditions of the order of probation, or may terminate such probation, when in the opinion of the court the ends of justice shall require, and when the probation is so terminated the court shall enter an order discharging the probationer from serving the imposed penalty; or the court may revoke the order of probation and cause the rearrest of the probationer and impose a sentence and require him to serve the sentence or pay the fine originally imposed, or both, as the case may be, or any lesser sentence. If imposition of sentence was suspended, the court may impose any sentence which might have been imposed. If probation is revoked, the time of probation shall not be taken into account to diminish the time for which he was originally sentenced.

(b) If a person violates a condition of probation by using a controlled substance or by failing to comply with prescribed treatment for the use of a controlled substance, the court may order, in addition to or in lieu of the actions and sanctions authorized in subsection (a) of this section, the temporary placement of the person in custody, when in the opinion of the court such action is necessary for treatment or to assure compliance with conditions of probation.

Source: http://www.dccourts.gov/dccourts/superior/index.jsp

District of Columbia Courts: http://www.dccourts.gov

Washington:

Revised Codes of Washington Section 9.95.230:

Court revocation or termination of probation.

The court shall have authority at any time prior to the entry of an order terminating probation to (1) revoke, modify, or change its order of suspension of imposition or execution of sentence; (2) it may at any time, when the ends of justice will be subserved thereby, and when the reformation of the probationer shall warrant it, terminate the period of probation, and discharge the person so held.

Source: http://apps.leg.wa.gov/RCW/default.aspx?cite=9.95.230

Washington State Courts: http://www.courts.wa.gov

West Virginia:

West Virginia Code of Criminal Procedure §62-12-11. Probation period.

The period of probation together with any extension thereof shall not exceed five years. Upon the termination of the probation period, the probation officer shall report to the court the conduct of the probationer during the period of his probation, and the court may thereupon discharge the probationer or extend the probation period. Whenever, before the end of the probation period the probationer has satisfactorily complied with all the conditions of his probation and it appears to the court that it is no longer necessary to continue his supervision, the court may discharge him. All orders extending the probation period and all orders of discharge shall be entered in the records of the court, and a copy of all such orders shall be sent by the clerk of the court to the board within five days after the making of the order.

Source: http://law.justia.com/westvirginia/codes/62/wvc62-12-11.html

West Virginia Judicial System: http://www.state.wv.us/wvsca/wvsystem.htm

Wisconsin:

Wisconsin Statute Section 973.09(3)(a):

Wisconsin Statute Section 973.09(3)(a) provides that "prior to the expiration of any probation period, the court, for cause and by order, may extend probation for a stated period or modify the terms and conditions thereof."

Source: http://wilawlibrary.gov/topics/justice/crimlaw/probation.php

Wisconsin Court System: http://www.wicourts.gov/

Wyoming:

Title 7 - CRIMINAL PROCEDURE

ARTICLE 3 - PROBATION AND SUSPENSION OF SENTENCE

Wyoming Code of Criminal Procedure Section 7-13-304. Imposition or modification of conditions; performance of work by defendant.

(a) The court may impose, and at any time modify, any condition of probation or suspension of sentence.

(b) As a condition of any probation, the court, subject to W.S. 7-16-101 through 7-16-104, may order the defendant to perform work for a period not exceeding the maximum probation period.

(c) As a condition of probation or suspension of sentence, the court may require a defendant who is a minor to successfully complete a juvenile service program offered by a community juvenile services board under the Community Juvenile Services Act.

(d) As a condition of probation or suspension of sentence, the court may require a defendant to complete successfully a court supervised treatment program qualified under W.S. 7-13-1601 through 7-13-1615.

Source:

http://legisweb.state.wy.us/statutes/statutes.aspx?file=titles/Title7/T7CH13AR3.htm

Wyoming Judicial Branch: http://www.courts.state.wy.us/

V
Vermont 138
Virginia 139

W
Walton, Sam XXI
Washington, DC 139-140
Washington State 140
Westlaw.com 88
West Virginia 141
Will, George 81
Wisconsin XIX, 23, 53, 63, 64, 89, 141
Words of Wisdom XXI
Wyoming 142

Y
Answers.yahoo.com 86

Get Off Probation

Closing:

I wish each of you the best of luck in your efforts to get off probation and rebuild your life.

J Jones

www.getoffprobation.com

Photo Credits:

Cover Page: Breaking Chain: Source: istockphoto.com
V: Lady Justice, holding scales and a sword: Source: istockphoto.com
XIII: Scale of Justice: Creative Commons License, Wikipedia.
1: FAQS: Source: istockphoto.com
9: Contemplation of Justice: Source: Creative Commons License, Wikipedia.
79: Lincoln Monument: Source: istockphoto.com
89: Freedom Eagle: Source: publicdomainclip-art.blogspot.com
Back Cover: Breaking Chain: Source: istockphoto.com